Blank Fictions

**Consumerism, Culture and the
Contemporary American Novel**

James Annesley

Pluto Press

First published 1998 by Pluto Press
345 Archway Road, London N6 5AA

British Library Cataloguing in Publication Data
A catalogue record for this book is available from
the British Library

ISBN 0 7453 1091 5 hbk

Designed and produced for Pluto Press by
Chase Production Services, Chadlington, OX7 3LN
Typeset by Stanford DTP Services, Northampton
Printed in the EC by TJ International, Padstow

Blank Fictions

Carol, Brian, Sarah and Gavin

Contents

Acknowledgements

Special thanks to Pete Nicholls, Josh Cohen, Sarah MacLachlan, Tim Armstrong, Maria Balshaw, Liam Kennedy, Clive Bloom, Anne Beech, Ben Gill and Humphry Couchman. I must also thank my family for their patience and Karen for putting up with me.

Some of the material in this book draws upon previously published work. Parts from Chapter 2 originally appeared in 'Commodification, violence and the body: a reading of some recent American fictions', in Tim Armstrong (ed.), *American Bodies: Cultural Histories of the Physique* (Sheffield: Sheffield Academic Press, 1996) and 'Bret Easton Ellis', in *Post-War Literatures in English* (Groningen: Martinus Nijhoff, 1996). Portions of Chapter 5 formed part of 'What's going on: interdiscursivity, popular culture and American blank fiction', in *Overhere: A European Journal of American Culture* (Summer 1996), vol.1.1. Sections from Chapter 6 were originally published in 'Decadence and disquiet: recent American fiction and the coming *fin de siècle*', in *The Journal of American Studies* (Winter 1996), vol.30.3.

1

Reading the Scene

You might not be sure what it is, but you can be sure that it's out there. Turn on the TV and it's there. Go to the movies and you'll see it. Open a magazine and it'll be there. Flick through a rack of CDs and you'll find it. Turn the pages of a novel and you'll read it. You must have seen it, even if you're unable to name it. It's found in the images of excess and indulgence that dominate Larry Clark's *Kids* (1996). It's tangled up in the violence of Bret Easton Ellis's *American Psycho* (1991) and Dennis Cooper's *Frisk* (1991). It's part of confessional biographies like Jerry Stahl's *Permanent Midnight* (1995), Elizabeth Wurtzell's *Prozac Nation* (1994) and Catherine Harrison's *The Kiss* (1997). You can hear it when Beck sings 'I'm a loser baby ... why don't you kill me?' Common sets of themes are being articulated. There's an emphasis on the extreme, the marginal and the violent. There's a sense of indifference and indolence. The limits of the human body seem indistinct, blurred by cosmetics, narcotics, disease and brutality.

The contemporary American scene is littered with imagery of this kind and it's hard to escape the conclusion that culture is taking a new direction, exploring new kinds of experiences and moving towards new forms and subjects. Identifying this culture is one thing, but defining it or explaining it quite another. It's easy to recognise this scene, but harder to read it. This portrait of contemporary American culture can be developed by considering the specific implications raised by its preoccupation with violence, indulgence, sexual excess, decadence, consumerism and commerce. These obsessions, so much a part of the general flow of late twentieth-century culture, find a particularly precise expression in recent American writing and it is around these novels that the following discussions will revolve. Using examples drawn from modern fiction, the intention is to build up an understanding of the ways in which these different concerns

1

are articulated and to analyse these issues in terms that can be used to develop a wider perspective on the contemporary scene.

The increasing emphasis on violence, sexual experimentation, drug use and urban despair in recent American fiction thus provides the foundations for this project. With the emergence of the 'bratpack' in the 1980s, novels dealing with disaffection, decadence and brutality became familiar features in American publishing. Ten years on, with Bret Easton Ellis and Jay McInerney positioned as central figures in the literary establishment, stories of indolence, extremism and marginality have become staple elements in recent American fiction. Writers like Donna Tartt, Susanna Moore, Douglas Coupland, Sapphire, Katherine Texier, Mark Leyner, Ray Shell and Evelyn Lau have emerged behind the original bratpack to create a kind of writing that has been described in different terms, as the 'fiction of insurgency', 'new narrative', 'blank generation fiction', 'downtown writing', 'punk fiction' and, the term favoured here, 'blank fiction'.[1]

Shared among the majority of these writers is a desire to focus their work on the experiences of American youth (teen, twenty and thirty somethings). Their novels are predominantly urban in focus and concerned with the relationship between the individual and consumer culture. Instead of the dense plots, elaborate styles and political subjects that provide the material for writers like Toni Morrison, Thomas Pynchon and Norman Mailer, these fictions seem determined to adopt a looser approach. They prefer blank, atonal perspectives and fragile, glassy visions. This familial resemblance is strengthened by a common interest in the kinds of subjects that obsessed William Burroughs, Georges Bataille and the Marquis de Sade. They are, as Amy Scholder and Ira Silverberg suggest, preoccupied with 'sex, death and subversion'.[2]

Though it's difficult to argue that this group of writers constitutes anything as substantial as a literary movement, these continuities are supported by a common context. The New York of the 1980s is a central reference point for the majority of these writers. The clubs, restaurants and galleries of Manhattan brought Ellis and McInerney together and provided the material for their bratpack novels. Not only did they live in the same city during this period and know each other socially but they were also connected professionally by a network of agents, publishers and literary critics. New York-based magazines like *Between C & D* and *Bomb* extended these relationships and provided a link between the novels of the bratpack and the work of Joel Rose, Katherine Texier, Lynne Tillman, Gary Indiana and Dennis Cooper. Publishers like Grove and Weidenfield, Semiotext(e) and Poseidon added their support by backing the work of writers from this scene, a process that has been given new impetus in recent years with the expansion of the increasingly influential publishing house Serpent's Tail and the emergence of the High Risk imprint. Their successful promotion of Tillman, Indiana, Cooper and others has contributed greatly to the growing interest in novels of this kind. The relationships established by this infrastructure of magazines and publishers have been strengthened by the willingness of many of these writers to appear together in public readings. There is, quite clearly, both a common context and a common vision and, while there is no 'blank manifesto', these affinities suggest the existence of a 'blank scene'.

The coherence of this account of the emergence of blank fiction is not, however, reflected in the range of explanations that have developed around these texts. One view suggests that these disturbing thematics are the product of an 'apocalypse culture', the reflexive gestures of a society torn by millennial angst.[3] Other versions see a culture dominated by a 'Generation X', slackers whose indifference is reflected in the atomised, nihilistic worldview articulated in these texts.[4] An alternative account speculates about the possible existence of some kind of radical aesthetic that finds expression in extreme, marginal statements and pronouncements.[5] More familiar and, perhaps, more persuasive is the well-worn suggestion that this modern mood can be explained in relation to 'postmodern culture'.[6] Blank fictions are read, in these terms, as the product of a postmodern condition, their twists and turns interpreted as reflections of the material structures of late twentieth-century American society.

This range of interpretations shows that while there's a common sense that there is something out there, there seems to be little agreement on exactly how to read or conceptualise it. Arguments linked to the millennium and Generation X are too dependent on a loosely conceived modern zeitgeist to offer much in the way of critical rigour. The suggestion that this fiction is engaged in a radically transgressive project seems equally problematic. Celebratory in tone and reliant on an adversarial politics, this interpretation is strangely unsuited to the analysis of fictions that seem so blank and uncommitted. In contrast, an approach based on terms drawn from the postmodernism debate seems more substantial. Whether focused on the critical potential of what Linda Hutcheon calls 'historiographic metafiction' or reading these narratives in Jamesonian terms as cultural forms that 'replicate – reproduce – reinforce the cultural logic of late capitalism', this kind of argument focuses on the ways in which contemporary narratives articulate anxieties about subjectivity, representation and the relationship between text and context.[7] The problem with these approaches, however, is that they collapse the distinctions between different narrative forms and offer postmodernism as an all-embracing explanation. Arguments of this kind are unable to explain how novels that are very obviously looking to distinguish themselves from the canon of postmodernist fiction should find themselves grouped together beneath the same postmodern umbrella. To consider Bret Easton Ellis and Lynne Tillman in the same breath as Thomas Pynchon and Don Delillo seems misguided. This approach is weakened further by its tendency to read all recent cultural forms as the product of social and economic structures. Fiction, from this perspective, seems passive. Lost in the abstract sign-space of contemporary American culture, it is unable to offer anything more than a blank reflection of this 'cultural logic'. Postmodern culture thus becomes a catch-all, a category that is used in so many different circumstances that it loses its explanatory power.

Problematic though these interpretations may be, their shared grasp of the significance of period and context can not be brushed aside. It is this general sense of blank fiction's place in late twentieth-century American culture that must be central to any interpretation of it. The novels of Bret Easton Ellis, for example, resonate with the spirit of the age. An interpretation built on an analysis of the social currents and experiences of this particular period provides, it seems, the most sensible way of approaching the vision of an indolent, wealthy, white elite offered in *Less Than Zero* (1985) and his portrait of a murderous yuppie in *American Psycho*. This emphasis on the specifics of time and place is echoed by Tama Janowitz in *Slaves of New York* (1987) and Jay McInerney in his novels *Bright Lights, Big City* (1986) and *Brightness Falls* (1992). They, like Ellis, draw their material from the particularities of this period and offer images of the excesses of New York in the 1980s. The world of cocaine, Wall Street, exotic eateries and major-label suits provides the common reference point for these texts and fosters readings that interpret them in direct relation to the social, cultural and political dynamics of late twentieth-century American life. The politics of Reagan, deregulation and the free market are, it seems, neatly reflected in *Bright Lights, Big City* and *American Psycho*.

The problem with this interpretation is that it hinges on an approach that reads literature as a direct image of social conditions. The feeling is that these texts reflect their context, but such intuitions are, in Terry Eagleton's terms, 'too trimly symmetrical, unable to accommodate the dialectical conflicts and complexities, the unevenness and discontinuity, which characterise literature's relation with society'.[8] The relationships between literature and social conditions need to be interpreted in terms that go beyond models based on reflection. The point is, as Richard Godden makes clear, that any reading of literature focused on the 'relationship between the sign and existence in a group of novels must be preoccupied with exactly how existence gets into the sign'.[9] Interpreting the links between the material realities of 'existence' and the aesthetic structures of the literary 'sign' is central to an understanding of the connections between social context and the novel. These relationships are, however, too complicated to be explained in the appealingly straightforward terms offered by arguments based on either reflection or homology. An alternative approach can be developed by thinking briefly about V.N. Vološinov's formalist theory of literature.

In Vološinov's argument, though he agrees that literature has a strong and specific relationship with social life, he is determined to maintain a clear sense of the distinction between aesthetics on the one hand and material conditions on the other. In his terms, between transformations in social and economic structures and changes in the aesthetic lies 'a long, long road that crosses a number of qualitatively different domains'.[10] For Vološinov tracing the course of this road involves a concentration on language and an appreciation of the ways in which linguistic meanings depend upon particular material contexts. Meaning, in Vološinov's reading, is 'the effect *of interaction between speakers and listeners produced via the material of a particular social complex*'.[11] Semantics, he argues, depend as much upon cultural reference points as they do upon formal meanings. In these terms, a particular novel's style, structure and language can be seen to bear the marks of its context. The focus on these formal concerns provides, as far as Vološinov is concerned, an understanding of the connections between social life and literature and offers an insight into the mechanisms through which 'existence gets into the sign'.

Loaded with references to the products, the personalities and the places that characterise late twentieth-century American life, blank fiction is profoundly aware of its own time and place. This emphasis means that, despite anxieties about the usefulness of arguments based on mechanical readings of the relationship between literature and society, any attempt to move away from a contextual reading of these novels would be problematic. An analysis of the shape and character of late twentieth-century American social and material conditions would, with this in mind, appear to provide an appropriate foundation for any reading of this particular literary form. The point is, however, as Vološinov's remarks make clear, that the analysis of fiction in contextual terms demands an approach that does not look, straightforwardly, at the ways in which a novel depicts its own period, but concerns itself with the processes through which a text thematises contemporary conditions on structural, stylistic, linguistic and metaphorical levels.

These mechanisms can be traced by reflecting on blank fiction's constant allusions to retail outlets, brand names and styles. Bret Easton Ellis's novels typify this kind of approach. His characters don't drive cars, they drive 'BMWs', they don't eat in restaurants, they eat in 'Spago's', they don't wear sunglasses, they wear 'Raybans'. The range of mass cultural references not only characterises blank fiction, but also positions it very precisely in a particular time and place. Crucially, however, this sense of context is developed not through detailed description, or specific reconstruction, but through the text's incorporation of the commercialised products of a particular epoch. It's not dates that matter, nor is it situations or personalities, it's the commercial features of the environment that provide these novels with their reference points. Blank fiction does not just depict its own period, it speaks in the commodified language *of* its own period.

The privileged position given to the commodity in these novels thus establishes a clear sense of context. This contextualising function is strengthened by the relationship these references establish between blank fiction and wider economic and material structures. The incorporation of a range of commercial allusions doesn't just provide these novels with a spatial and temporal location, it also serves to link blank fiction to the dynamics of contemporary capitalism. This connection is important because it lays the foundations for an interpretation of blank fiction that reads these novels in relation to the historical processes of the late twentieth century. Instead of an approach based on the slippery categories and concepts of postmodernism, the suggestion is that a focus on the category of the commodity provides a way of interpreting blank fiction in terms that combine a strong sense of the significance of both period and place with a wider perspective on contemporary capitalist structures.

The fact that processes of commodification seem increasingly more central to the functioning of late twentieth-century capitalism adds weight to this argument. Running through interpretations of contemporary economics as diverse as Michel Aglietta's *A Theory of Capitalist Regulation*, Daniel Bell's *The Coming of Post-Industrial Society* and Alain Touraine's *The Post-Industrial Society* is a consistent emphasis on the significance of the commodity.[12] Their arguments dwell not only on the key role played by consumerism in contemporary capitalism, but also on the ways in which this modern capitalist period can be defined by its ever intensifying levels of commodification. This perspective is shared by Ernest Mandel who, in *Late Capitalism*, argues that contemporary economics involves a 'vast penetration of capital into the spheres of circulation, services and reproduction', a process that operates 'by extending the boundaries of commodity production.'[13] Relentless commodification, a process that effects almost all levels of social life, characterises what he calls the 'late capitalist' period. For Mandel, 'the age of late capitalism ... drives ... the capitalist mode of production to its highest pitch.'[14]

This focus on commodification in late twentieth-century society is important because it can be connected to a sense of the significance of commodities in blank fiction. Using a language that seems to resonate with the accents of commercial culture, these texts develop formal dimensions that appear, in some cases commodified and in others, part of a wider engagement with consumer culture. They are novels that seem to dramatise Mandel's vision of a society in which capitalism is operating at its 'highest pitch'.

The emphasis on the different ways in which these texts represent commodification is supported by the complex functioning of the category of the commodity itself. Following the work of Pierre Bourdieu it is possible to recognise the ways in which it serves a dual function. As Bourdieu argues, the commodity has both an economic significance and an expressive social function. In this respect, the commodity plays roles that are simultaneously economic and cultural, articulating, as Robert D'Amico suggests, both 'an exchange value and a *hieroglyphics* of cultural relations'.[15] The commodity becomes a 'way of seeing in contemporary America', offering insight into both cultural and economic patterns.[16]

Commodification thus provides the focus for an examination of both the specific features of this kind of writing and an interpretation of the relationships between its shape and character and the wider context of late twentieth-century culture. Though the privileged position accorded to the commodity in the following discussions is based on an understanding of both the importance of commodification in late capitalism and the stress these novels place on these particular formations, there is no sense in which the commodity is being offered as a 'master category', or some kind of 'last instance'. Social context is not being employed as a metaphysical absolute against which all ideas and cultural products must be measured. Instead the aim is to use this approach to develop one way of reading this kind of fiction. The intention is to offer a perspective on blank fiction that is aware of its relationship with historical conditions and to produce an interpretation that shows how those conditions are seen, registered and known in recent American narrative. This concentration on the function of the commodity thus provides a way of reading the contemporary scene.

In the chapters that follow, the characteristics of blank fiction will be explored in terms that keep a continual eye on the relationship between these fictional elements and the processes and trajectories of consumerism and contemporary capitalism. A focus on blank fiction's preoccupations with violence, sexual extremes, decadence, commerce and mass culture will offer insights into both the implications raised by these particular elements and also a sense of the ways in which these components interlock. The different dimensions in these novels seem to produce a variety of perspectives on the contemporary scene and it is this range of inflections that will provide the substance for the discussions that follow.

This attempt to unite a fictional form as seemingly loose and empty as blank fiction with these materialist perspectives might seem, however, at first glance, like a rather perverse project. David Lehman's comment that the works of Ellis and McInerney possesses all 'the intellectual nourishment of a well-made beer commercial' typifies the generally dismissive response to fiction of this kind.[17] These novels are seen as light, empty and commodified with the implication being that they are of little 'value'. Crucially, however, in identifying these writers with the commercial culture of advertising Lehman provides a clue to unlocking their wider significance. Connecting blank fiction to a beer commercial may be appropriate, but to dismiss it because of that relationship is to miss the point. In an age of infomercials, product-placement and ambient advertising, writers who are tuned into the dynamics of commodification must inevitably be able to provide important insights into the contemporary scene. The irony is that in dealing with supposedly lightweight and ephemeral elements these texts manage to engage with the kind of weighty material forces that are fundamental to the whole functioning of late twentieth-century society. In a commercial world understanding the relationship between subjectivity and commodification is crucial. Blank fiction may well be like a 'well-made beer commercial', but it can still provide a surprising amount of 'intellectual nourishment'. As subsequent chapters will try to show it is the blank, empty and commercial nature of these novels that, in a paradoxical fashion, opens up a way of conceptualising contemporary conditions and turns the process of saying a little into the act of disclosing a lot.

2
Violence

Even before the publication of *American Psycho*, Bret Easton
Ellis's writing had divided opinion. Having been acclaimed for
his best-selling debut *Less Than Zero* and then pilloried after
the much-publicised failure of his second novel, *The Rules of
Attraction* (1987), he was well-acquainted with the vagaries of
literary celebrity. The extremes which had characterised his
career up to that point could not, however, have prepared him
for the extraordinary response provoked by *American Psycho*.[1]
Even before publication, the book made waves when Simon
and Schuster, the publishers of his first two novels, decided
to terminate his contract. Alarmed by what they saw as the
novel's disturbing and distasteful subject matter, they refused
to publish, leaving Ellis free both to negotiate a new deal with
Random House and to keep his $300,000 advance. Though
remarkable in themselves, these events provided a mere prelude
to the outrage that greeted the publication of the book itself.
Vilified as a 'how to manual on the torture and
dismemberment of women', the novel seemed to attract
condemnation from all sides and even prompted *The New
York Times* to insist that its readers 'snuff this book'.[2] The few
critics who did try to defend the novel tended to privilege issues
linked to censorship and freedom of speech over criticism of
the text itself, an approach that strengthened the impression
that *American Psycho* was more of a literary event than a work
of literature. Needless to say, the publicity produced by these
controversies made *American Psycho* Ellis's most successful
book to date and guaranteed him a place in the history of
American literature.

Central to the furore generated by the publication of this
novel is a fundamental anxiety about the representation of
violence in contemporary culture. The murders committed by
Patrick Bateman provide the focus for Ellis's text and form the
central image of American psychosis. The problem is, however,

that much of the criticism that has surrounded the novel has been founded on two basic misconceptions about the significance of its representations of violence. On one level commentators have failed to see the distinction between the views of the author and the activities of his character. The pleasure Bateman derives from violence is interpreted as an expression of Ellis's own sadism. The result is that the moral censure that should be applied to his literary character falls instead upon the author. Ellis, they argue, has written a novel that celebrates and encourages violent behaviour.[3] This desire to collapse the boundaries between Ellis and his creation is exacerbated by a more general confusion over the relationship between images of violence and real violence. Overlooking the basic distinction between art and reality, too many commentators have confused the significance of representations of murder with the meaning of actual murders. What these arguments fail to appreciate is that the relationship between a literary image of violence and violence itself is at best tenuous and at worst non-existent. Violence in literature serves a complex symbolic and communicative function. Any analysis of violent imagery in contemporary American narrative must try to consider the implications raised by this reliance on the expressive possibilities offered by the language of violence.

What makes the controversy aroused by *American Psycho* seem even more perplexing is that Ellis's portrayals of brutality are neither unusual nor unprecedented. The gruesome scenes and violent images offered in his narrative are not shocking deviations from the mainstream, but elements that are, in fact, characteristic of it. This widespread emphasis on representations of violence can be seen in, for example, the films of Abel Ferrara and Quentin Tarantino, Jonathon Demme's *Silence of the Lambs* (1990), Raymond Carver stories like 'so much water so close to home' (1977) and 'Tell the women we're going' (1981), Ray Shell's and Jess Mowry's tales of urban deprivation and drug dealing, the Vietnam novels of Bobbie Ann Mason, Jayne Anne Phillips and John Nicholls and the revisions of Western mythology offered by Clint Eastwood in *Unforgiven* (1992) and Cormac McCarthy in *Blood Meridian* (1985). The existence of general patterns of violence in recent American culture undermines the effectiveness of critiques aimed at singling Ellis out as a uniquely corrupting influence. The fact that brutal images are as familiar to the American imagination as the narratives of Jack London, Edgar Allan Poe and Ernest Hemingway makes this response even more incomprehensible. This censure seems particularly confusing when considered in relation to the specific details of the novel itself and the way in which Ellis orientates his text around an obviously moral position.

American Psycho is narrated by Patrick Bateman, a twenty-six-year-old Wall Street broker, New York socialite and serial killer. The novel moves through a series of partially connected sequences in which the extremes that characterise Bateman's life become increasingly apparent. In order to understand the novel's moral trajectory it is important to appreciate the ways in which Ellis establishes powerful links between the society of mass consumption and Bateman's brutality. In the terms laid down by Ellis, Patrick Bateman's murders are crimes for which an increasingly commercial and materialistic society must take ultimate responsibility. Though on the surface Bateman's crimes seem motiveless, it is his rampant consumerism that provides the key to understanding his activities. The commercial nature of Bateman's desires is dramatised in a scene in which he describes how

> In an attempt to understand these girls I'm filming their deaths. With Torri and Tiffany I use a Minox LX ultra-miniature camera that takes a 9.5mm film, has a 15mm f/3.5 lens, an exposure meter and a built in neutral density filter and sits on a tripod.[4]

In this section Bateman seems unaware of the difference between commodities and human life. He slides from his 'attempt to understand' the lives of his victims into a long and overly technical description of his possessions. The tone he uses mimics the register of a commercial brochure and he appears to have lost the ability to differentiate between his casual and abusive treatment of human life and a jargon-studded analysis of his electronic toys. His desire to catalogue is so overpowering that it infects his whole personality and inspires not only tedious, itemised lists of his property, but also intensely detailed descriptions of violence. The litany of atrocities constitutes, like his discussion of his camera's specifications, some kind of reflection on the power of his ownership. Bateman is a consumer with unlimited desires and as such he is unable to distinguish between purchasing a camera and purchasing a woman. The violent treatment of his predominantly female victims is thus tied to his vision of a world in which everything has been commodified.

Ellis strengthens these impressions by developing his portrait of Bateman's personal identity and producing a character for whom personal wealth and personal identity are one and the same thing. People are measured by the amount they earn, the clothes they wear and the places they eat.[5] The judgements he makes are based on economic valuations. In one scene, for example, he is able to categorise a haircut as 'bad because it is cheap'.[6] In another, he condemns the woman who works in his local video store because the shoes she wears are 'maddeningly ... only sneakers – *not* K-Swiss, *not* Treton, *not* Adidas, *not* Reebok, just cheap ones'.[7] These details reveal a character who is unable to differentiate between material things and human life. This confusion not only infects his response to the people around him, but also the way he thinks about himself. In Bateman's internal monologues, his patterns of thought mix emotions and commodities:

> Shirt from Charivari. Fusilli I am thinking. Jami Gertz I am thinking. I would like to fuck Jami Gertz I am thinking. Porsche 911. A Sharpei I am thinking. I would like to own a Sharpei. I am twenty-six years old I am thinking. I will be twenty-seven next year. A Valium. I would like a Valium. No *two* Valium I am thinking. Cellular phone I am thinking.[8]

The obsession with ownership dominates his reflections on his personal well-being. His psychic dilemma is lived out in a world of consumer items and expressed in a fragmented range of desires that includes a lust for Jami Gertz, the need to buy a Porsche and acquire a Sharpei. This relationship between

identity and a frenzied consumerism fosters an aggressive
jealousy in Bateman. He can not bear to see someone with
something that *he* has not got without finding himself
overwhelmed by murderous urges. In one section Bateman
arrives at a restaurant in tears because he is convinced he will
not be able to get a good table.[9] In the same scene he has to
fight to control his anger when confronted by the sight of a
colleague's newly prepared and obviously expensive business
card. These trivial events seem to provoke Bateman and stir
his violent temper. In one part of the novel his jealous response
to Paul Owen's career success is so extreme that it leads,
ultimately, to Owen's murder.[10]

These petty jealousies are grounded on the comparisons
Bateman makes between himself and others in terms of
ownership. The motivations for his crimes are thus firmly
located within the material realm. The role played by
consumerism in Bateman's activities is not, however, limited
to motivation. Bateman's crimes are both inspired by his
consumerist lust and also predicated upon his wealth. As
Bateman himself observes, he is 'rich – millions are not', an
advantage that equips him with the tools he requires to
commit his murders, the money he needs to buy his victims
and, significantly, the power to purchase the legal protection
required to avoid imprisonment.[11] The text shows Bateman
paying off his victims and financing his defence against what
he calls some 'bogus rape charges'.[12] He uses his money to
cover the marks made by his consumerist brutality.

Consumer capitalism and personal wealth thus provide the
central reference points for Ellis's American psycho. This
impression is strengthened in a section that sees Bateman
playing word games with his job-description and twisting the
phrase 'mergers and acquisitions' into 'murders and
executions'.[13] This grisly slip-of-the-tongue is echoed in the
pun on the name of Bateman's Wall Street company with
'Pierce and Pierce' referring both to the owners and to a
repeated act of violent penetration.[14] The conscious blurring
of the distinctions between buying and selling stocks and
shares and the objectifications of murder set the pattern for a
novel in which the metaphorical image of the cut-throat
dealer is turned into a reality.

The parallels established between Bateman's excessive consumer lusts and his violence underlines these impressions. In his desperate desire to consume the latest foods in the latest restaurants and to discover increasingly rarefied and exclusive tastes, Ellis finds an image of consumption that combines consumer urges with much more obviously corporeal desires. Bateman consumes both economically and physically, spending his money while satisfying his palate. The word consume is thus used in all of its possible meanings: purchasing, eating and destroying. These three meanings converge in Bateman's sexual murders, a point dramatised when Bateman travels to

> the meat-packing district just west of Nell's, near the Bistro Florent to look for prostitutes ... I find her on the corner of Washington and Thirteenth. She's blond, slim and young, trashy but not an escort bimbo ... And behind her, in four-foot-tall red block letters painted on the side of an abandoned warehouse, is the word MEAT.[15]

This passage not only objectifies the woman in terms of her 'MEAT', but makes more subtle connections between Bateman's obsession with new commodities and his violence. The scene is located in relation to one of Bateman's favourite restaurants with the implication being that this woman represents, quite simply, just another physical sensation for him to enjoy. In his consumerist imagination her body promises to provide a pleasure akin to the rare foods he finds in 'Bistro Florent'. Thus, when in a later chapter Bateman tries 'to cook and eat [a] girl', he is not only expressing his violent lusts, but articulating a confused consumerism that has run out of control and exceeded all boundaries.[16] Bateman's inability to control his consumerist desires thus functions as an image of a society in which everything is for sale. As far as Bateman is concerned, his desire is sovereign and his purchasing power the ultimate arbiter. The principles of the free market are thus taken to their most extreme conclusion with Bateman's crimes serving a hyperbolic function. Using this hyperbole, Ellis draws out the contradictions of the free market system and shows the ways in which it finds itself in conflict with moral values.[17]

Ellis reinforces these ideas by positioning Bateman within the world of the broker and connecting him to the terrains of electronic finance, telecommunications and international dealing. This environment, as Mark Poster suggests, is one in which

> The word 'money' now refers to a configuration of oxides on a tape stored in a computer department of a bank. The connection between the oxides and the function of the exchange medium is arbitrary, revealing its socially constituted character, and the representational aspect of 'money' is sustained through language ... its referent being remote and difficult to discern. The case of 'money' illustrates the great elasticity of represented language, the way words refer to things that are at a very great remove from them, but also the limits of that elasticity. The next step in linguistic change is the formation of the simulacra.[18]

Central to Poster's analysis is his sense of the ways in which these electronic processes erode the concrete referentiality of finance. In this environment the abstract valuations represented by money are taken to an even higher level of abstraction. The referent of hard currency is replaced by computer digits and 'oxides on a tape'. Marx discussed money in terms of its ability to represent pure commodification, but he maintained a sense of money as some kind of concrete token. In the sphere of electronic finance it is not simply the economic referent that is 'remote and difficult to discern', but the sign itself that has been derealised.

This process of derealisation takes on a crucial role in *American Psycho* because Bateman's inability to relate to any kind of reality seems to fuel his violence. Bateman's work on Wall Street, his daily encounters with computer screens spilling digits with only a tenuous connection to the concrete values they represent, has created, in the terms of the novel, a sense of financial and material unreality that weakens his grip on the real. The result is that Bateman becomes unable to see his actions in anything other than fictional terms. Thus, in the

Isolating himself.

same way that his manipulations of money are separated from the material realities they represent, his violence seems equally unconnected to either human experiences or humanity.

Ellis supports this impression by connecting these abstracting processes to the simulations constructed by the mass media. These relationships are developed in descriptions of Bateman that establish a sense of the ways in which he experiences his life as if he was living in a film or a TV show. Using a language patterned with movie jargon, Bateman's narration incorporates phrases like 'a slow dissolve', 'smash cut' and 'jump zoom'.[19] A more overt sense of this filmic self-conception is provided in a section that sees Bateman describing how he is 'used to imagining everything happening the way it occurs in the movies, visualising things falling somehow into the shape of events on the screen'.[20] Bateman is, in a very literal sense, screened off from reality: he gets his economic data from the computer screen; his understanding of life in New York from the glimpses he sees of the world through his limousine's smoked-glass windscreen; his cultural information from the media. This screening, in classically Baudrillardian fashion, appears to restrict his ability to distinguish between reality and illusion to the extent that his violent acts become, in his imagination, indistinguishable from the unreal images he sees around him. In a confessional moment he admits to having dreams 'lit like pornography in which I fucked girls made out of cardboard'.[21] This admission creates the impression that these media experiences have infiltrated his imagination to the extent that he is unable to differentiate between real sexual violence and fantasy. The fact that he makes such an effort to film the suffering of his victims adds to this impression and suggests that, as far as he is concerned, these acts are simply an extension of what he perceives as his right to generate, project and consume images. He is unable to see the misery created by his behaviour because he lives his life in a world that has become as unreal to him as TV. The irony is that if, as the novel suggests, this video-violence has dulled his ability to understand human relations and has, as a result, fostered his brutality, then the act of filming his victims makes further atrocities more likely.

Ellis's representation of a technologically mediated world thus inclines towards a Baudrillardian reading of contemporary society in terms of hyperreality and simulation. Ellis's character inhabits a world in which his dominant experiences are derived through the media. The consequence is that the criteria for distinguishing simulation from reality are lost leaving Bateman trapped in an environment in which everything is grounded on his own projections and fantasies. For the author, it is this media culture that must take part of the blame for Bateman's atrocities. Ellis's argument is that the contemporary's culture of images and signs creates the conditions in which Bateman's violence and indifference can flourish. In Ellis's imagination, the madness of Patrick Bateman is the natural product of a society in which rampant consumerism intersects with the hyperreality of a media society. The nightmarish activities described are thus intended to satirise this confluence of forces. In this respect, Ellis can be seen to be trying to bring an ethical critique to bear on the conditions he describes. As Elizabeth Young suggests, Ellis's work presents 'terrible moral deviations, which, if rectified, would restore to society all the moral values it has lost and would revive a more wholesome dominant culture'.[22] He fears that the process of commodification and the loss of the referent through the proliferation of simulations will erode all traces of humanity and create a culture of emptiness and indifference, a culture anthropomorphised in the figure of the American Psycho.

Ellis adds to this disturbing vision by presenting Bateman not as some horrific aberration, but as a yuppie everyman. He is, as far as his elite acquaintance are concerned, essentially normal.[23] It is not just that he 'looks pretty much the same' as everybody else, or that he wears the same clothes, shops in the same stores and seems to share the same values, it is, more alarmingly, that he is '*total GQ*' and a complete conformist.[24] This normality makes his actions seem even more horrific, a horror that is emphasised by the absence of any kind of existential reflection on his own behaviour or any desire to legitimate it in psychological terms. There is no effort to represent Bateman's activities as destructive attempts to define himself in terms of a nihilistic personal gesture like those imagined by Albert Camus in *L'Etranger* (1942) or André Gide in *Les Caves du Vatican* (1950). His murders do not represent some kind of *acte gratuite* but are left as hollow and inexplicable acts of violence. The failure to supply an existential background is compounded by Ellis's silence on Bateman's family history and personal past. This approach closes down the possibility that the reader could explain Bateman's behaviour in relation to either his experiences or his relationships.[25] This approach enables Ellis to create a text that makes society responsible for Bateman's crimes. He is not killing to define himself, or killing because of some childhood trauma, but killing purely and simply in terms that respond to the forces of the mass media and the free market.

The novel thus offers a rigid explanatory perspective on Bateman's behaviour. Ellis is trying to arouse moral indignation and inspire a critical response to contemporary capitalism and media institutions. In these terms, *American Psycho* can be read as a novel with an intensely moral agenda. Ellis's point is that the human dimension has been occluded in contemporary society with destructive consequences. The result is, as Elizabeth Young suggests, that Ellis offers a vision that is ultimately 'conformist and conventional. He is skilled at representing disintegration ... and his energies are straight-forwardly judgemental and condemnatory.'[26] What makes Ellis's judgemental approach interesting is that it generates powerful contradictions within the text. When, for example, Ellis sets out this clear satirical design, he takes it for granted that the world he depicts, the culture of commodification, simulation and sign games, exists in the way he says it does. He does not, however, take into account the possibility that this representation of late twentieth-century society might involve specific kinds of distortion. Ellis constructs an *image* of modern America, not a statement of fact. His failure to question his own model can, as a result, work against his intention and actually reinforce the ideological foundations of the cultural conditions he is trying to interrogate. From this perspective, it is possible to argue that the culture Ellis attacks is as much a product of his own imagination as a reflection on real conditions in late twentieth-century America.

If this reluctance to contemplate the accuracy of the model of society he depicts is one of the key weaknesses in Ellis's text, then wider problems can be brought to light by thinking about the way in which *American Psycho* represents the culture of the image. If this culture, and in particular the culture in which images of sex and violence are commonplace, is seen to be partially responsible for Bateman's brutal activities, then surely the images offered in the text can, in the same way, be seen to contribute towards these destructive processes. Ellis's text, with its graphic representations of sexual murder must, by implication, be condemned by the text's own logic and attacked for its use of what are, in the terms of the novel, elements that are morally problematic, potentially damaging and dangerously influential. Ellis may be using these representations to make a point about sex and violence in contemporary culture, but in doing so he produces a text that employs those representations in a way that mimics the very processes he is criticising. Ellis's censorial attitude does not, it seems, extend to include the graphic scenes that provide the cornerstones for his own text. This is particularly ironic considering the history of the publication of the novel. Having been saved from a censorial publisher, Ellis's text has entered the public sphere to promote a more restrictive and moralistic attitude towards images of sex and violence.

This contradiction can be linked with features in the text that reveal its fundamental dependence upon the forces of commodification. Ellis's general target may be late twentieth-century capitalism, but the text's reliance on a language filtered from the world of commerce and its continual emphasis on the styles and activities of the financially privileged discloses a connection between the novel and these economic formations that runs contrary to the trajectory of its critical project. *American Psycho* is immersed in the commodified world of late twentieth-century culture to the point where its efforts to criticise that world seem problematic. Ellis's apparently satirical representations of Bateman's long monologues on the benefits of specific facial products or the quality of Evian water are aimed at underlining contemporary society's trivial obsessions, while actually producing a narrative that reflects those tendencies and obsessions. These contradictions are compounded by the way in which Ellis's rigorous antagonism towards contemporary society limits his text's range and flexibility. If, as Ellis's argument seems to suggest, the objectifications of consumer society are responsible for Bateman's behaviour, then this novel in a sense shadows that process of objectification in both its fixed view of New York society and its endlessly detailed portraits of consumer objects, acts of consumption and, most importantly, violent murder. Ellis himself seems to offer a frozen, or reified image of the contemporary, a literary strategy that reflects the mechanisms of commodification itself. *American Psycho* can thus be read as a text that participates in the processes of commercialisation and objectification that were the very forces it set out to satirise.

In *American Psycho* Ellis offers violence as a metaphor for the processes of commodification that are infiltrating, objectifying and cutting up the social body of late twentieth century America. The proliferation of media simulations throughout contemporary society is seen to encourage these violent acts, with the novel's implication being that commercial culture, in all its manifestations, is dangerous and destructive. What makes Ellis's work particularly interesting is the extent to which other writers can be seen to share his vision of a brutalised society. *American Psycho* is not an aberrant text, but one that has clear parallels with a number of contemporary American narratives. In, for example, Brian D'Amato's novel *Beauty* (1993), a similar sense of malaise is generated through the novel's concentration on images of bodily violence. Though *Beauty* concentrates on the controlled medical violence of cosmetic surgery rather than the random destruction of the serial killer, both novels use the image of the brutalised body as a metaphor for a society that is being mortified and carved up.

D'Amato's *Beauty* tells the story of Jamie Angelo, a New York sculptor who forsakes the art world to become an unlicensed cosmetic surgeon. Angelo is a dealer in beauty, an individual whose career shadows that of Ellis's murderous broker. Bateman and Angelo inhabit the same kind of world, the Manhattan of cocktail parties and new restaurants and coke in the washrooms. Throughout the novel, Angelo experiments with new and untested techniques that allow him radically to alter the faces of his female customers. As the narrative progresses, his skills develop to the point where he is able to give his girlfriend, Jaishree, a face that brings her work first as a model and then as a supermodel. This dreamlike progression turns sour when the side-effects of his operations begin to take effect and his creations turn on their creator. At the end of the novel D'Amato's Frankenstein is forced to confront the rage of the monstrous beauties he has fashioned.

The significance of beauty in D'Amato's novel is central to the meanings generated by the text. The focus on the body's aesthetic establishes a series of links between the individual human body and the economic body. Beauty is both a received judgement on the body's appearance and a means of putting an economic valuation on that appearance. When Angelo transforms Jaishree's face, he dramatically increases her earning power. The complex functioning of the idea of beauty thus positions the body within the exchange system and provides the means through which it is transformed into a commodity.

Traditional interpretations of beauty have tended to focus on its links with spiritual well-being. Ralph Waldo Emerson described it as the 'mark God sets upon virtue', while John Keats identified a link between beauty and truth.[27] Veblen, however, challenged these romantic readings of beauty with a materialist account that connected the 'ideal' of feminine beauty to 'pecuniary strength'.[28] In Mark Seltzer's terms, 'Veblen's theory ... anticipated ... the notion of the female body as a sort of leading economic indicator of consumer culture'.[29] It is this intersection between economic forces and the corporeal that provides the focus for D'Amato's text and generates the tensions between the self and the social that are established in its representations of the surgically altered body. These slickly performed procedures represent brutalisation. Jamie Angelo attacks the flesh, penetrates it, cuts it and moulds it into new shapes. Despite the controlled violence of these operations, D'Amato is at pains to emphasise the quality of the results achieved. Angelo does not perform minor alterations, he completely restructures faces. The crude cosmetic surgery of silicon and liposuction is replaced by a fantasy surgery that

can transform the human frame. Central to the narrative is the
sense that cosmetic surgery provides a means of marketing and
commercialising the body's appearance. Beauty, supposedly
'free' and 'natural' is, as a result of cosmetic surgery,
transformed into a product that can be bought by those with
sufficient financial resources. D'Amato's text describes a
situation in which beauty is put up for sale in absolute terms.
The fantasy operations D'Amato depicts are freed from the
constraints imposed on real cosmetic surgery by factors like
age and bone structure. The only thing *Beauty*'s surgical
procedures need is money.

It is, of course, important to acknowledge that the
connection between money and beauty is not unique to a
world in which the kind of complete transformations described
by D'Amato are possible. Cosmetic surgery is nothing new. The
histories of foot-binding and infibulation, for example, give
a sense of the antiquity of practices intended to adjust the
body's appearance.[30] More importantly, the cultural norms
that define the beautiful face must be read in terms that
appreciate the formative role played by the taste of dominant
power groups. Veblen see these links in particularly clear
terms, recognising that in

> the constricted waist which has had so wide and persistent
> a vogue in the communities of Western culture, and also the
> trained foot of the Chinese ... are mutilations of
> unquestioned repulsiveness to the untrained sense ... Yet
> there is no room to question their attractiveness to a society
> into whose scheme of life they fit as honorific items
> sanctioned by the requirements of pecuniary respectability.[31]

For Veblen, the aesthetic perception of the female body
responds to wider forces of economic authority and social
hierarchy.

It is possible, however, to argue that the kind of practices
described in *Beauty* establish links of unprecedented strength
and directness between economics and the body. The situation
D'Amato creates is one in which the body, and specifically the
female body, is totally fetishised. The perceived balance
between the natural and the social represented by the body is

thus upset by processes that see the body being increasingly controlled by the forces of commodification. In the conditions envisaged by D'Amato the body is overwhelmed by economic concerns. These processes echo Marx's reading of commodification and offer a very precise image of the dehumanising consequences of commodity fetishism.

> The mysterious character of the commodity form consists therefore simply in the fact that the commodity reflects the social characteristics of men's own labour as objective characteristics of the products of labour themselves, as the socio-natural properties of things.[32]

Marx's position finds a specific resonance when read alongside D'Amato's text, prompting recognition of the ways in which his novel represents cosmetic surgery as a process of dehumanisation that is both abstract and physical. In *Beauty*, what D'Amato calls the 'tyranny of aesthetics' is such that identity is made to hinge on appearance with the result being that it becomes more dependent on the physical form than on its lived dimensions.[33] In the same way that labour finds itself solidified in social terms, identity is frozen in the body's image. The fetishisation of the body's aesthetic appearance is such that it dominates lived experience and transforms them into 'objective characteristics'. For Marx, the objectification of labour takes place on the level of social psychology. In D'Amato's text this abstract process is translated into a corporeal event. The narrator is seen operating on his customers, literalising the fetishising process by converting their bodies and objectifying their identities in ways that have a specific price. These processes are dramatised in a scene that shows Angelo spending the night with the newly transformed Jaishree and finding himself 'seized by a wave of revulsion, as if I was sleeping with a dead thing'.[34] The 'dead thing' is, quite literally, a commodity, frozen and stripped of its human dimensions. The dehumanising impact of fetishisation is thus exactly paralleled by the dehumanising effects of surgically brutalising the body. All the consequences of commodification identified by Marx are thus present in this system. In his terms, the consequences of the commodifying process is that the 'social relation between men themselves ... assumes ... the fantastic form of the relation between things'.[35] The difference is, however, that in D'Amato's text this economic process involves an added level of dehumanisation that takes place in a way unforeseen by Marx. *Beauty*'s bodies are commodities both on an abstract level and in literal terms.

D'Amato's representations of cosmetic surgery's economic penetrations into the body thus offer an image of an increasingly commodified world. Cosmetic surgery is one of the branches of 'body maintenance' that, according to Mike Featherstone, provide 'an expanding market for the sale of commodities'.[36] In this way the novel offers a representation of the increased intensity of economic activity, the heightened levels of commodification, that characterise the late capitalist period. Like Mandel, both Featherstone and D'Amato seem to recognise that late twentieth-century economics depend upon an acceleration and extension of the market and place a particular emphasis on the ways in which those principles have reached into and commodified the body. In Jameson's reading of late capitalism, he argues that this period is defined by a 'prodigious expansion of capital into hitherto uncommodified areas'.[37] This 'expansion' involves a colonising, penetrating process in which, as Jameson suggests, 'the last vestiges of nature which survived into classical capitalism are at length eliminated'.[38] In this description of the economic encroachment into the 'last vestiges of nature' lies a very precise image of exactly the kinds of mechanisms depicted in *Beauty*, processes that see cosmetic surgery as a dehumanising, brutalising procedure that commodifies the human frame.

The relationship between this economic model and D'Amato's text can be developed by considering the central role played by aesthetics in the promotion of products. D'Amato dramatises this function in his portrayal of Angelo's search for the supposedly perfect face. His energy is concentrated on an attempt to construct a composite image of different looks using the already commodified images of fashion models and film stars. In one episode he sifts through a 'batch of color laser Xeroxes of beautiful women from painting and sculpture through the ages', while in another he is shown scanning pictures from *Vogue*, *Glamour* and *Elle* and using them to produce a template of a 'make-believe woman' whom he hopes 'could really represent all Woman'.[39] He takes these airbrushed, idealised images of beauty as the models for his own creations, transforming them into a new kind of commodity. This triumph of commodification means that these advertising devices become products in their own right. D'Amato's artist-surgeon thus takes advertising images and turns them into realities in the faces he constructs. A perfectly commodified system results with the product and the promotion melding into one. Capital, in D'Amato's world, instead of selling through advertising, now sells advertising itself. The circle closes completely when the women who have been transformed using images from fashion and the cinema become themselves fashion models and film stars. In one scene, D'Amato captures this circularity in graphic terms by describing Angelo's visit to a department store and his encounter with mannequins that have been modelled on one of *his* surgically transformed women. He writes:

> One day I went shopping in Barney's ... there was a whole gang of her there, unmoving, five garishly swim-suited, variously wigged clones, staring down at me with lifeless eyes through the window. Apparently a mannequin company had made a head design based on her; kind of an interesting reverse switch, I guess, but I kind of lost interest in shopping that day.[40]

This is not a case of life imitating art, but a case of life imitating advertising with that imitation then being transformed once more back into promotional material.

The importance of beauty to the processes of product promotion has long been established. In *Critique of Commodity Aesthetics*, W.F. Haug identifies the 'aesthetic illusion' as the key element in the marketing process and argues that 'within the commodity system of buying and selling, the aesthetic illusion – the commodity's promise of use value – enters the arena as an independent function of its selling'.[41] In D'Amato's novel the women who have had their faces transformed are not just the products and the customers, but are also the advertising. A cosmetic surgeon's clients are living advertisements for that surgeon's skills. In Haug's view, this cycle of commercialised images is a central part of the marketing process. His suggestion is that 'aesthetic innovation, as the functionary for regenerating demand, is thus transformed into a moment of direct anthropological power and influence'.[42] Rachel Bowlby offers a similar kind of interpretation when she argues that 'the commodity makes the person and the person is, if not for sale, then an object whose value and status can be read off with accuracy in terms of the things he has and the behavioural codes he adopts'.[43] The commodity's transformative potential is, in Bowlby's terms, associated with the aesthetic illusions supplied with the commodity. This transformative potential is made real in D'Amato's text which represents the 'anthropological power' of the advertising image in a way that sees those images being themselves anthropomorphised.

One problem with this reading is, however, that it relies on assumptions that figure the body in ways that contradict more established critical positions. The suggestion here is that the penetration of the body represents a diminishment of human experience. Corporeal limits are signalled as precious and the breakdown of those limits marked in negative terms. This contradicts the orthodox line which places the piercing of the body's limits in a positive light by arguing that such denaturalisations disrupt the body's perceived unity and undermine positions that draw their strength from biologically determined reasoning. Recent criticism has made a great deal of, for example, the significance of the female cyborg, interpreting her as a figure that dramatises the artificiality of the construct of the body.[44] A cyborg's prosthetic organs are read as an expression of her ability to define herself and her own body rather than having her body defined for her. These approaches do not, however, work well when linked to the denaturalising effects of cosmetic surgery represented in *Beauty*, where the surgical processes seem to enforce dominance rather than deconstruct it. In the kind of procedures described in *Beauty*, the penetration and transformation of the body work to reproduce cultural norms. The women created are not cyborgs, but mannequins. Rather than breaking up culturally constructed ideas about the female body, this kind of cosmetic surgery carves those constructions deeper into the skin.

The interrelationships D'Amato constructs between the commodity, the commodity's image, the consumer and the body thus offer a perspective on the complex functioning of the economic in late twentieth-century society. D'Amato's text represents the body as a site in which a number of conflicting forces meet. It is the consumer and the consumed, the selling point and the product. The fact that the dehumanising consequences that attend the body's commodification take effect in ways that allow the objectified body to become an aesthetic illusion and thus complicit in its own objectification is one of the most striking twists in D'Amato's argument. The roles played by violent transformation, brutalisation, exploitation and commodification in D'Amato's text make these twists even more interesting and provide a link between the kind of deadening effects described in *Beauty* and *American Psycho*'s images of objectification. Both novels see late twentieth-century society as a place characterised by heightened levels of commodification, an intensification which carries violence and dehumanisation in its wake.

Beauty's brutal representations of cosmetic surgery and *American Psycho*'s descriptions of a murderous broker establish a range of clear connections between violence and consumerism. Opportunities for interpreting the depictions of bodily violence in Dennis Cooper's novel *Frisk* seem, in contrast, much more limited. Cooper's writing, like that of both Ellis and D'Amato, combines slick stylistic surfaces with resolutely violent material. Unlike them, however, *Frisk* lacks the overt emphasis on consumerism.

Based in Los Angeles, Cooper's work first appeared in local 'zines and small magazine publications like *Between C & D* and *Bomb*. The publication of *Frisk*, *Closer* (1992) and *Try* (1994), brought him a much wider American readership and increased both his profile and his influence. *Frisk* focuses on the lives of a group of young, gay, Californian men. The novel describes them sleeping with each other, acting in porn films, prostituting themselves and taking drugs. The central character and narrator, Dennis, is haunted by a teenage memory of a brutal pornographic photograph. This image of an apparently dead boy preoccupies him throughout the novel and provides a touchstone for his obsessions with masochistic sex and murder. At the end of the novel Dennis moves from Los Angeles to Amsterdam. The penultimate section of the book contains a long letter written by Dennis to a former lover. The letter describes a series of sexual murders that he claims he and two accomplices have committed while in Holland. Dennis's accounts of these murders represent the human body in a completely objectified and dehumanised manner. One typical section describes the treatment of a corpse in the following terms:

> We cut him apart for a few hours and studied everything inside the body, not saying much to one another, just the occasional, Look at this, or swear word, until there was nothing around but a big, off-white shell in the middle of the worst mess in the world. God human bodies are such garbage bags.[45]

There is no sense here that the corpse is in any way connected to human life. It is just a thing to be mutilated, it is the 'worst mess in the world'. This inhumanity is heightened by the lack of communication between Dennis and the other murderers. They just grunt at each other, swear and make phatic observations. The mix of revulsion and boredom is typical of Cooper's style. He explores the dark recesses of human experience with a literary technique that Roger Clarke has likened to a 'gold endoscope'.[46]

Economic resonances in this kind of writing are not immediately apparent. Traces of the commercial can, however, be found in the way Cooper's text objectifies the body. The language of transforming living matter into dead echoes Marxist interpretations of commodity fetishism as a kind of metaphorical death. As Georg Lukács argues, 'the individual object ... is distorted in its objectivity by its commodity character'.[47] In his terms, the 'transformation of a human function into a commodity reveals in all its starkness the dehumanized and dehumanizing function of the commodity relation'.[48] These dehumanising processes are shadowed by the 'distortions' performed by Cooper's murderer.

This position is strengthened through the novel's emphasis on the connections between these murders and coprophilia. This relationship emerges in a dialogue that develops between Dennis and his punk victim:

> I'd never wanted to eat someone's shit before, but I was starved for the punk's. I asked him if it had been eaten before. He mumbled, No, let me go. I asked him if he'd like me to eat it. He said, Are you really going to kill me? I said No very casually. Then I repeated my question. He said he didn't know what I meant. I said if he'd shit in my mouth we'd let him go. He said okay.[49]

The tone of this description, with its emphasis on the way everything was done 'very casually' and the sense of Dennis's apparent indifference creates a kind of screen around the events. It is possible, however, to cut through this screen by concentrating on the way in which the piece connects commodification, excrement and murder and interpreting them in terms drawn from Norman O. Brown's discussion of 'filthy lucre' in *Life Against Death*. Brown's position is that 'money is inorganic dead matter which has been made alien by inheriting the magic power which infantile narcissism attributes to the excremental product'.[50] These relationships between excrement and money are reflected in *Frisk*'s description of Dennis's attempt to bargain with the punk. Dennis, employing a system of exchange based on excrement instead of money, encourages the punk to try to buy his freedom with his 'filthy lucre'. This commercial proposition commodifies the punk's body while simultaneously devaluing it by pricing it in excremental terms. The point is that this devaluation takes place on both literal and metaphorical levels as the body is simultaneously subjected to the abstract mortifications of the reifying process and the real mortifications of sexual violence. The casual brutality described in *Frisk* is thus linked to a dehumanising transaction that generates 'dead matter' in economic terms (the commodity), in psychological terms (excrement) and in real terms (murder).

This sense of the relevance of Brown's ideas can be developed by considering the ways his argument moves towards a reflection on what he identifies as the fundamental human need to produce objects that are both 'alien' and 'dead'. Brown writes:

> Excrement is the dead life of the body, and as long as humanity prefers a dead life to a living, so long is humanity committed to treating as excrement, not only its own body, but the surrounding world of objects, reducing all to dead matter and inorganic magnitudes.[51]

Brown's understanding of humanity's commitment to treat 'as excrement ... the surrounding world of objects' gestures towards a parallel between his position and Marx's interpretation of commodification's objectifying impact. The problem with this relationship is that Brown's work is resolutely ahistorical. His argument reads this tendency to reduce everything to 'dead life' along essentialist lines and suggests that there is 'something in the structure of the human animal which compels him to produce superfluously'.[52] The ahistoricism of Brown's stance can be broken down, however, by putting a historical slant on his attempt to locate history's meaning in individual psychology. Brown's suggestion that surplus is produced in response to an essential human impulse can be projected onto a historical axis and reinterpreted as a manifestation of the intrinsically overproductive character of capitalism. The historicisation of Brown's thesis thus creates an opportunity to develop these ideas on death, excrement and the body into a wider reflection on the dehumanising and objectifying forces of commodification. This approach enables *Frisk's* representations of coprophilia and violence to be viewed in a way that illuminates the increasingly dehumanising conditions generated by the intensified levels of commodification in late capitalism. The parallels between Brown's argument and the imagistic scheme employed by Cooper prompt a recognition of the economic dimensions in *Frisk* and thus provide a framework for interpreting the text's repeated emphasis on scenes that involve the transformation of living matter into dead.

The opportunities for reading *Frisk*'s representations of the body in these economic terms can be extended by examining the text on a more straightforward level. Like the commercial focus developed in *Beauty*'s descriptions of cosmetic surgery, *Frisk*'s depictions of pornography and prostitution are full of commercial resonances. In *Frisk*, as it was in *Beauty*, the aesthetic illusion of the commercialised body is both an economic valuation and a corporeal attribute. Once again evaluation of the body's physical appearance and assessments of its beauty are seen to lock the human frame into a network of commercial relationships. In porn acting the beauty of the body marks the value of the performer. In a similar way, the aesthetics of the body determine the worth of the prostitute. Pornography and prostitution are not, of course, new types of commercialisation and it is difficult to argue that they, in themselves, represent an intensification of economic activity in the contemporary period. What is important in *Frisk*, however, is the way these professions dominate. Everybody sells their body in the accelerated flesh-market Cooper portrays.

This reading of the violent imagery in *Frisk* must be tempered by an appreciation of the fact that the murders described are in fact nothing more than the product of Dennis's imagination. His letter is a fiction and nobody really gets hurt. Even the 'snuff' photograph that has such a significant effect on his imagination is shown to be a fake. In this respect *Frisk* appears to be a novel that gestures towards familiar postmodern concerns about the ontological status of fiction. The consequence is that the material perspectives offered in this analysis seem to be at odds with a text that is apparently intent on interrogating the whole problem of the relationship between materiality and representation. This is the line Elizabeth Young takes in her essay 'Death in Disneyland':

> Cooper's central concern is something that has obsessed postmodern theorists. Faced with a seamlessly hyperreal society, apparently invulnerable to negation or political change, theorists have struggled to articulate a 'real' that escapes representation.[53]

Young's Baudrillardian reading locates Cooper's work within the aesthetic flux of postmodern writing and implicitly rejects interpretations grounded on material concerns. The fundamental problem with this approach, however, is that Young is unable to step outside the boundaries of postmodern thought and remains caught up in exactly the kind of hyperreality she describes. Cooper is forced to replicate Baudrillard in a way that leaves his postmodern pronouncements unchallenged, a process that traps *Frisk* in a cyclical logic in which fiction can only reflect on a 'seamlessly hyperreal' world. A materialist reading of these fantasies, on the other hand, breaks down this sense of hyperreality and allows *Frisk* to be read in terms that interpret the social significance of its fantasies.

It is possible to strengthen this position by considering the way Cooper's text, in combining the brutal with the banal, seems itself to invite reflection on the meaning of these relationships. The glossy character of *Frisk*'s style, a style that enables Cooper to move smoothly between the horrific and the mundane, works to generate specific anxieties about the meaning of violence and the status of the body. The text's blank response to corporeality compels the reader to reflect on this blankness and encourages a search for the elements that have been displaced in the narrative's attempt to appear empty. In Young's terms, 'to Cooper, the body itself is a text; it is a "problem" to be "read" ... like "braille"'.[54] The concern is, however, that in emphasising the abstractions of textuality Young fails to take into account the material nature of Cooper's writing. In these terms, *Frisk* needs to be interpreted, not as a self-reflexive text about the representation of the body, but as a novel which actually concerns itself with the relationship between writing and materiality.

These issues are explored in clearer terms in Cooper's short narrative *Jerk* (1993). *Jerk* describes a puppet show being staged as part of a drama course. In a manner typical of Cooper's writing, the show depicts violent death. These representations of violence are complicated by the fact that Cooper's puppeteer is an individual who is himself a murderer. One part of the text reads:

Between the murders he has committed and the artistry informing his puppetry lies a path so overly complicated by his obsessional need to reconstruct his participation that the actual meaning is subsumed by it, almost the way the libretto is dissolved in the music of an opera.[55]

It is the link between the artistry and the representation of the murders that is important here, a relationship that, the text suggests, is so heavily weighed in favour of the aesthetic that it can almost dissolve the events, like the music dissolves the libretto of an opera. These concerns are developed in the piece's final section, a movement in which one of the show's audience writes a report on what he has seen. In this report he comments on the puppeteer's motivations and suggests that

Without privileged access to moral codes through which his crimes acquire meaning, his perception of them remains mediated by an encroaching emotion, compounded by his current sense of meaning, which is less about finding new things than seeing things anew.

Perhaps these crimes would have disappeared with abstraction had the puppeteer not, at an irreversible moment of sexual energy, attempted to understand them, and thereby awaken a childish response which refused to yield to the formalist unity he now requires of his act. For while the puppets have emerged, they merely confront his understanding with a hermeticism that is impossible to break open.[56]

The idea of 'seeing things anew' places the emphasis on artistic form and focuses the discussion around concerns linked to the tensions between his 'abstraction' and his 'crimes'. At the heart of these problems lies the 'hermeticism' of violence, a hermeticism that is not only 'impossible to break down', but actually capable of confronting, challenging and destabilising the puppet show's 'formalist unity'. These violent scenes slip, or are jerked, outside the limits of the text and bring a horrific range of elements into play.

In this reading Cooper's texts seem to 'frisk' and 'jerk' through and around these violent experiences creating dynamics which are, in many respects, too dark and disturbing to be fully comprehensible. The result is a tension between the smooth, slick surfaces of Cooper's writing and the brutal realities they depict. In these terms Elizabeth Young is right to link Cooper's work with Barthes's sense of *'jouissance'* and correct to identify the extent to which his texts are, in Barthes's terms, 'fresh, supple, lubricated, delicately granular'.[57] The looping fantasies in *Frisk*'s early chapters and the interlocking narratives that mix the narrator's imaginings with a description of his own experiences create the impression of a text that is running beyond its limits into the kind of blissful freedom conceived by Barthes. The only problem with this emphasis on the text's shimmering membrane is, however, that it fails to grasp the bloody realities protruding through this stylistic skin.

The logic of *Frisk* suggests that death is 'strictly a sexual fantasy, a plot device in certain movies', but the reader is constantly forced to question these dismissive perspectives.[58] The result is a narrative that produces a powerful disjunction between its slick, depthless style and its relentlessly material subject matter. In these terms the novel's representations of the body can be seen to play a crucial role in the process of breaking through the surface of the text and exposing the violent, material experiences lying underneath. Thus, in his violent descriptions, Cooper finds a way of connecting his fluid style onto a material framework. According to Barthes, the pleasure of the text develops as 'it granulates, it crackles, it grates, it cuts, it comes' and in many ways Cooper would appear to agree.[59] The key difference is, however, that Cooper uses this style as a process that allows him to disclose the presence of the material in violent moments that rupture the text's blissful surface.

This approach differentiates Cooper's work from that of both Ellis and D'Amato. Where Ellis, for example, finds himself describing the violence of commodification using a literary technique and narrative voice that seem to have been reified, Cooper develops a much more subtle and slippery kind of approach. Unlike Ellis, he is not intent on taking a strong satirical line, but determined instead to explore contemporary conditions with an inquisitive eye. This tone is sustained by the complexities of Cooper's textual organisation, a structure that creates narrative loops that are in turn contained within further loops. Cooper's tone is consistently casual. The text skims over details and is littered with dismissive phrases like 'this part's a blur' and 'Oh, who cares anymore'.[60] It is Cooper's focus on violence, however, that provides a very obvious connection between his work and that of both Ellis and D'Amato. All of them share anxieties about reification in its different forms and all of them have a sense of the ways in which the body is being incorporated and commodified.

These readings of violence are thus located within a framework of ideas linked to the analysis of commodification in late capitalism. *Frisk*, *Beauty* and *American Psycho* employ images of the brutalised body to develop a wider perspective on dehumanisation, objectification and reification. This interpretation of the blood-letting depicted in these three novels gestures towards the possibility of establishing a wider perspective on modern American narrative's general preoccupation with violence, an understanding that sees in this preoccupation a reflection on the relationships that connect violence, commodification and the body. The representations of violence offered by these three authors are thus read in terms that move away from a straightforwardly literal interpretation. Violence in these novels is not read in direct relation to violence in American society, but considered in abstract terms and taken as a metaphor for the deadening impact of commercialisation in the late twentieth century. The following chapter's examination of the representation of sex in blank fiction will extend these ideas and consider the ways in which this emphasis on commodification can be used to explain, not only the proliferation of violent imagery in recent fiction, but also its increasing emphasis on acts of extreme sexuality.

3

Sex

Aligned with the representations of violence that characterise many blank fictions is an emphasis on scenes of explicit sexuality. For Cooper and Ellis, in particular, violence is often linked to extreme sexual experiences. Their narratives are, it seems, as concerned with sex as they are with death, a preoccupation that finds its fullest expression in the descriptions of sexual murder that pattern the pages of their novels. This relationship is important because it provides the basis for an approach that reads this emphasis on explicit sexual material in terms that reflect the implications raised by the representations of violence. The connections between sex and violence suggest that the interpretative perspective offered on brutal imagery might be adapted and reapplied to produce a reading of blank fiction's sexually explicit elements. In the same way that it was possible to interpret literary images of violence in terms that identified them with the commodified currents of late twentieth-century American life, opportunities seem to exist for a similar kind of approach to blank fiction's representations of extreme sexuality. The presence of a strongly exhibitionistic streak within the general patterns of contemporary American culture adds legitimacy to this perspective.

Mainstream American cinema's willingness to deal with subjects that dwell on the industry of sexual display provides one obvious reference point for this discussion. Films like *The People Vs Larry Flynt* (1997), *Showgirls* (1996) and *Striptease* (1996) make exhibitionism one of their central concerns. Like Hollywood, smaller productions have also moved into this terrain. Gus van Sant's *My Own Private Idaho* (1991), Steven Soderberg's *sex, lies and videotape* (1989), Atom Egoyan's *Exotica* (1994) and *The Adjuster* (1991), Hal Hartley's *Amateur* (1995), Denys Arcand's *Love and Human Remains* (1993) and Larry Clark's *Kids* are all narratives in which pornography, prostitution, striptease and sexual experimentation serve a crucial narrative function.

Like contemporary cinema, the general currents of recent American fiction seem equally preoccupied with sex. Kathy Acker's explicit explorations of sexuality and Mary Gaitskill's reflections on sado-masochism in *Two Girls Fat and Thin* (1991) are all familiar enough. Less well-known might be Dale Peck's self explanatory *Fucking Martin* (1993), Jane Delynn's *Don Juan in the Village* (1990), Pagan Kennedy's *Stripping* (1994) and Poppy Z. Brite's *Lost Souls* (1992). More recently still, Kathryn Harrison's confessional tale *The Kiss*, Jennifer Belle's *Going Down* (1997) and Candace Bushnell's unimaginatively entitled *Sex and the City* (1996) have all attracted considerable amounts of attention.[1] Like fiction, cultural theory also seems to have taken this 'sexual turn'. Camille Paglia's *Sex, Art and American Culture* (1993), Dorothy Allison's *Skin: Talking about Sex, Class and Literature* (1995) and Elizabeth Grosz's and Elspeth Probyn's collection *Sexy Bodies* (1995) all, in one way or another, attempt to theorise sexuality in terms that shadow the preoccupations of both film and fiction. Even this discussion can be interpreted within this context. Like these other texts, it must, inevitably, contribute to this sexual turn even as it commentates upon it.

Sexually explicit images and themes are thus, it appears, characteristic of the contemporary scene. Sex is, of course, not a new subject and there is no sense in which these elements are historically unique. What makes the contemporary situation interesting, however, is the extent to which this fascination with sex has permeated mainstream culture. Graphic depictions of sexual acts have, in previous generations, been the traditional domain of either avant-garde movements or commercial undergrounds. In the late twentieth century, however, sexual imagery can be found on the screen of any cinema and on the shelves of any bookstore.

The obvious interpretation of this cultural fascination with sex argues that the constant presence of these elements functions as an expression of some wider social obsession with all things sexual. From one side this sexual turn is regarded as the product of an increasingly decadent and immoral culture, while, from the other, it is said to symbolise wider political and imaginative freedom. The consequence is that critical coverage of these cultural products becomes entangled in arguments dominated by a praise/blame couple. The debate generated by Madonna's *Sex* (1992), a publication that provides further evidence of the sexual turn in contemporary American culture, typifies the polarised responses inspired by material of this kind. For some, *Sex* is 'pornography', a word that, when used in this context, functions as a short-hand for everything that is immoral, exploitative and oppressive.[2] For others, however, Madonna's book is worthy of celebration. Linda Grant in *Sexing the Millennium*, for example, suggests that *Sex* offers a vision of 'some future sexuality'.[3] In terms that shadow established readings of Robert Mapplethorpe's work, a photographer whose influence on *Sex* can be discerned in almost every one of Steven Meisel's images, Grant interprets Madonna's sexual displays as radically transgressive acts that undermine convention and refuse domination. It is necessary, Grant suggests, to interpret Madonna's explicit gestures in ways that see the connections between sexual freedom, artistic freedom and social freedom.

This reading of visual culture has parallels with interpretations of contemporary writing. For many, the sexually explicit subject matter of recent writing functions in a way that reflects the issues raised by Madonna's *Sex*. Anna Powell, for example, interprets the presence of 'sado-masochism, bondage and domination, drugs and ultra-violence' in recent fiction as elements that 'offer possibilities at once disturbing and potentially liberating'.[4] In similar terms, Gregory Bredbeck reads the explicit sequences in contemporary American queer fiction as elements that work 'to expose the pervasiveness of hegemony.'[5]

The problem with these perspectives, however, is that they seem to offer a very narrow analysis of the sexual turn. American culture's fixation with all things sexual must be read in terms that go beyond interpretations tied to taste, censorship and cultural value. Such approaches are weak because they fail to take into account the ways in which these determined attempts to control the body, to strip away its protective layers and manipulate its movements, seem to speak of a culture in which the need to objectify is of paramount importance. A discussion of the representations of sex in Susanna Moore's novel *In The Cut* (1995) provides an opportunity for considering these processes in greater detail.

In the Cut is narrated by Frannie, a New York college lecturer whose life becomes involved in a series of violent sexual murders. With its gruesome subject matter and its flat, casual tone, the novel seems to have a lot in common with the blank fictions of Ellis, Cooper and D'Amato. The difference is, however, that where they set out to consider the relationships between violence and the body, Moore seems more concerned with exploring desire and sexual fantasy. With graphic images of sex pushed to the fore and a focus on the narrator's enjoyment of brutalising sexual experiences, the novel attracted a predictable amount of controversy. In terms that drew parallels with the debate generated by the publication of *American Psycho*, *In the Cut* was criticised for being deliberately provocative and dismissed as 'one of a growing number of American books and films to celebrate masochistic decadence'.[6] This concentration on the novel's seemingly shocking subject matter inevitably narrowed the debate and moved the focus away from many of the more complex issues raised by Moore's representations of sex. Provocation certainly plays an important role in the novel, but these sensationalist elements need to be considered within the terms of the text's wider engagement with the links between explicit sexuality, objectification and power.

In the Cut is centred around the relationship that develops between Frannie and Malloy, the detective in charge of the murder investigation. Their affair is constantly shadowed by the brutality of the murderer. Frannie is not only an important witness but also, it seems, destined to be the murderer's next victim. Against this macabre background Moore paints a series of graphic sexual scenes. In one typical episode Moore writes:

> He sat up and put an arm around my waist, turning me over and pulling me toward him so that I was on my knees, my ass high against him, his hand at the small of my back,

holding me to the bed. My face pressed into the bed. My arms stretched above my head. He pulled my arms to him ...[7]

The most striking thing about this description is the stress Moore places on Malloy's determined attempts to organise, position and arrange Frannie's body. There is a strong sense of Malloy's mastery here. He pushes her, presses her face into the bed and controls the movement of her arms. This emphasis on physical control is strengthened by the parallels established between the actions of Malloy and those of the murderer he is pursuing. The murderer's crimes are characterised by his need to dismember the bodies of his female victims by cutting them apart at the joints. These 'disarticulations', these attempts to control the limbs of his victims, reflect the actions of Malloy as he manipulates Frannie's body. Frannie's developing suspicion that Malloy might in fact be responsible for the crimes he has been assigned to investigate gives this sense of the murderous nature of Malloy's sexual behaviour an even more substantial dimension. The disarticulations performed by the murderer are thus very clearly reflected in the text's focus on Malloy's desire to twist and turn Frannie's limbs and on the concentrated attention he pays to parts of her body. 'Waist', 'knees', 'ass', 'hand', 'small of my back', 'face' and 'arms' are all listed in what is a resolutely anatomical descriptive passage. Moore's terse, unadorned prose adds to this impression and leaves the reader with the feeling that Frannie is being dissected and objectified on a physical level by her sexual partner, on an imaginative level by the murderer and on a stylistic level by the author.

A closer examination of *In the Cut*'s explicit content provides a way of clarifying this sense of the relationship between objectification and the text's emphasis on sexual imagery. Moore offers images of Frannie in which she seems to undergo a process of reification as she becomes a sexual object to be controlled, owned and consumed by Malloy. This reifying process can be placed in sharper focus by looking at a description of a sexual encounter between Malloy and Frannie that takes place inside the offices of the homicide department. The sequence begins:

He locked the door.

I stood with my back to the desk, watching him, unsure.

He unhooked a pair of handcuffs from their resting place on his belt and slid them noisily across the desk ...

'You're under arrest,' he said.

'What did I do?'

'You don't know?'

'Shouldn't I be arresting you?'

'I don't think so,' he said.

He turned me around and bent me over the desk, yanking my skirt around my waist ....

'That's right,' he said ... 'Give it up.'[8]

The sense of Malloy's mastery is once again prioritised in this description. Malloy incarcerates Frannie. He locks the door and displays his handcuffs. The fact that these events take place inside the police department office reinforces his authoritative position. He is very obviously in control, a power that is emphasised in his declarative 'You're under arrest' and the imperative 'give it up'. As was the case in the previous passage, these elements provide this section with a very strong sense of the ways in which Malloy dominates Frannie's body, a domination that is reflected in Moore's hard, flat representation of the scene.

This focus on *In the Cut*'s reified images of the body can be developed by reflecting on the economics of Frannie's relationship with Malloy and considering the ways in which their liaison can be seen to depend upon a sexual transaction. The terms of this bargain can be traced in an examination of Frannie's masochistic desires. For Frannie, surrendering herself to Malloy's authority produces a profound erotic charge. When she is in Malloy's office, his role as the keyholder seems to excite her, a pleasure that she strengthens by dwelling on the possibility that Malloy might be some violent Bluebeard ready to disembowel her at a moment's notice. Frannie's fantasies are fuelled by the reality of Malloy's sexual behaviour. Frannie is penetrated violently by Malloy, instructed to 'give it up' and told that she 'liked ... it'.[9] Throughout this scene and in others, it is clear that Frannie is deriving pleasure from masochism. What makes her masochism interesting is that, as Gilles Deleuze argues in 'Coldness and cruelty', masochistic desires are tied very strongly to bargaining and the process of establishing what Deleuze calls a set of 'contractual relations'.[10] In his analysis of Leopold von Sacher Masoch's *Venus in Furs* (1870), Deleuze concentrates upon the way the text offers images of sexuality that are linked to notions of property and objectification. This prompts Deleuze into an analysis of the connections between masochism and ownership and leads him to suggest that these relationships are grounded on an economic premise. Masochistic liaisons depend, like all good business deals, on the bond, the title-deed and the promise to pay.[11]

As is the case with *Venus in Furs*, the descriptions of masochism in Moore's text also seems to generate a range of commercial resonances. When, for example, in this scene in the police building, Moore depicts Frannie masochistically embracing Malloy's violent desires, the transaction is conducted in an office and takes place across the top of a desk. The implications raised by this location are strengthened by the inclusion of Frannie's observation that 'when I turned to go, I saw that the blotter on Captain Corelli's desk was stained'.[12] The bodily fluids created by their 'negotiations' have left their mark and, following established business practice, the bargain has been brokered and the contract has been signed, stamped and sealed with both parties delivered successfully to orgasm.

Moore's emphasis on these frozen tableaux of explicit sexuality finds its fullest expression in the novel's closing sections, in which Frannie is drawn into a series of encounters that lead her towards the ultimate mortification of death. In this conjunction of sex and death, Moore sketches out a series of relationships that underline the clear link between objectifying processes and these graphic sexual images. The events that lead to Frannie's murder begin when she handcuffs Malloy to a chair and has sex with him. In this scene, their conversation focuses on Frannie's 'worth', with Malloy confronting Frannie with the words 'You know what's wrong with you? You know your worth. You know just how much you're worth'.[13] This focus on Frannie's value, her price, sharpens when, on looking through Malloy's pockets for the keys to his handcuffs, she comes across an item of jewellery belonging to one of the murderer's victims. With her suspicions of Malloy seemingly confirmed, she flees her apartment, leaving Malloy chained up, and seeks help from Rodriguez, Malloy's partner. Rodriguez drives her out of the city and takes her to a deserted lighthouse. As they travel, it dawns on Frannie that it is not Malloy who is the killer, but Rodriguez. With Malloy left handcuffed in her apartment, she has no protector and the novel ends with Rodriguez murdering her. As he cuts her, she experiences death in sexual terms, observing that

> My skirt was heavy with blood, pooled between my thighs, seeping slowly through the cotton. It tickled when it dripped onto my skin, into my pubic hair, over the labia. I was not wearing any underwear.[14]

Even in her final moments she finds herself stimulated by the mixing of pleasure and pain. This sequence emphasises her objectification, detailing her clothing and her sensations. Crucially, as she describes the movement of the blood over her body, she shifts away from using 'my' to 'the', a change that takes place as she feels the blood touch the centre of her sexual arousal, 'the labia'. It might be *her* skin and *her* pubic hair, but her body seems distant and impersonal, transformed into an object by these violent sexual experiences.

In this way the novel establishes a relationship between its explicit descriptions and objectification. That Frannie should find herself unable to seek Malloy's protection from Rodriguez because she has chained him to a chair complicates these issues still further. Reversing the masochistic bargain by objectifying Malloy instead of allowing him to objectify her has fatal consequences. The sexual contract is underwritten in blood, a deal that cannot be broken or overturned. The novel thus establishes a connection between graphic depictions of sexuality and objectification, a link that provides a way of thinking about Moore's sexual turn in relation to these wider processes of reification.

These objectifications can be seen, not only in Moore's concentration on the concrete and material nature of the experiences she describes, but also, though perhaps less obviously, in her emphasis on the visual. *In the Cut* is a novel in which the sexual act and the acts of looking and seeing are interdependent. This relationship is dramatised during Frannie's last sexual encounter with Malloy, a sequence in which the focus on Malloy's desire to watch Frannie during sex is made clear. He agrees when Frannie tells him 'you like watching', and insists that she let him watch her reach orgasm.[15] In this section Malloy demonstrates a characteristic desire for powerful visual experiences during sex. Throughout the novel his sexual encounters with Frannie involve a strong sense of the importance of the spatial arrangement of her body. She must be positioned for best effect.

Malloy's voyeuristic preoccupations and the novel's emphasis on graphic physical experiences, dissection and objectification thus gives the piece a visual, almost cinematic quality. Frannie seems to see herself through Malloy's eyes. He plays the role of the director, her limbs are the props and he is intent on organising the posture of her body. This physicality is echoed in Moore's declarative style. Things are, for Moore, as they appear. She names and positions, but neither describes in depth nor attempts to look below the surface. The consequence is a novel that seems dominated by visual perceptions. Moore's work can, with this emphasis on the spatial and the visual in mind, be regarded as a type of writing that reflects the processes and techniques of the cinema, a kind of fiction that is in Joshua Cohen's terms 'cinematographic'.[16] Developing the arguments offered by Alan Speigel in *Fiction and the Camera Eye*, Cohen considers the relationship between cinematic and literary styles. Central to his argument is an emphasis on 'the flattened, derealised surface of the image', a 'flat denotative function' that reproduces the viewpoint of the camera eye.[17]

Cohen's discussion of this cinematographic flatness fits well with the analysis of a blank fiction like *In the Cut*. The 'denotative function' of the camera provides a template for the neutral records of events made by Moore, a model that can be strengthened by considering the ways in which this sense of the cinematographic seems to illuminate not only *In the Cut*, but also many other blank fictions. As the previous chapter has suggested, *American Psycho* is narrated by a character who sees the world in cinematic terms. Similarly, the fictions of Cooper and D'Amato seem to incorporate this stylistic flatness and write in ways that emphasise 'the derealised surface of the image', processes that reflect both the cinematographic elements identified by Cohen and the stylistic approach favoured by Moore. The implication is that this sense of the cinematographic provides a wider perspective on the flat styles and neutral viewpoints that characterise blank fiction as a whole. With *In the Cut*, however, Moore's fiction doesn't simply incorporate the techniques of the cinema, it also seems to reproduce the kind of objectifying effects that have long been identified as a feature of the cinematic gaze. The kind of aggressive visual and spatial organisation described by Moore echoes André Bazin's suggestion that the cinema relies upon a tyrannical perspectivalism.[18] The sexual objectifications that are such a central part of Moore's novel can thus be linked to these cinematic forces and conceptualised in terms that see a relationship between the novel's style, its emphasis on the visual and concerns related to power, control and objectification. In these terms the sexual turn dramatised in Moore's novel can be connected to a general emphasis on the visual. It is this relationship between sexual imagery and what Martin Jay calls the 'occularcentric' principle in contemporary culture that demands further examination.[19] The suggestion is that the exhibitionistic streak in American culture can be connected to the frenzied search for visibility that characterises so much of late twentieth century American society.

This sense of the way *In the Cut* brings together the sexual and the cinematographic seems to invite, almost inevitably, a reading that links the text's concerns with those of established interpretations of the ways in which the female body is objectified by a patriarchal gaze. From this perspective, *In the Cut* begins to look like a novel that is engaging with the kinds of debates theorised most famously by Laura Mulvey in 'Visual pleasure and narrative cinema'. Frannie's place as the object of both Malloy's and the murderer's attentions has clear parallels with Mulvey's analysis of the ways in which the female figure on the cinema screen is fetishised by the gaze of the male spectator. Further support for this parallel can be found in an understanding of the ways in which Moore's sharp, declarative prose pins the image of the body down on to the page in a manner that again reflects Mulvey's vision of the frozen figure of the female. This discussion of the objectifications of the visual elements in Moore's novel can be extended by relating it to *In the Cut*'s thematic engagement with issues related to reification. This emphasis on objectification does not, however, necessarily gesture towards a link with patriarchy. An alternative view can be offered by suggesting that these forces depend as much on capitalism as they do on the male gaze. Legitimation for this approach can be found in Mulvey's own work. 'Visual pleasure and narrative cinema' is an essay that employs a terminology drawn from writing related to commodity theory. In her argument, the gaze turns the body into 'the fetish object', a transformation that suggests the existence of a link between these objectifying processes and commodification.[20] Her use of a language borrowed from commodity theory makes the two approaches compatible, a symmetry that provides the foundation for an argument that sees the fetishising gaze as a function, not of masculinity, but of contemporary capitalism. The suggestion is that these visual objectifications have as much to do with the commodifying processes of late twentieth century economics as they do with the mortifications of patriarchy.

In this way, the kinds of sexual activities described by Susanna Moore are read as elements that have specific economic resonances. The text's representations of the reifying effects of the gaze seem to construct a vision of a commodified sexuality. It thus appears that the novel's sexually explicit elements can be interpreted in terms that owe more to materialist perspectives than they do to gender criticism. This materialist approach can be placed in a wider context by considering how the ideas raised in the discussion of this particular novel can be interpreted in terms of a general understanding of the links that bind the visual to the economic. The suggestion is that the connections established between graphic depictions of sexuality and commodification in Moore's novel be regarded as images of the way in which it is possible to regard the act of visualising and the act of looking as forces that are fundamental to the functioning of capitalism itself.

As the discussion of Brian D'Amato's *Beauty* has already made clear, the visual facilitates the general operations of capitalism by promoting demand. Just as the visual constructs the social, it can also be seen to organise and produce consumer behaviour. The appearance of a product, as Haug's *Critique of Commodity Aesthetics* suggests, is a crucial element in the process of product promotion. The visual provides a driving force behind the production of a desire to consume and thus, by prompting consumption, adds fuel to the whole process of production itself. If these processes are important to capitalism in general then there is a case for arguing that they must be even more important to late twentieth-century capitalism. This is a period in which economic processes are operating at their 'highest pitch'. Levels of commodification are accelerating and new markets being penetrated with an increasing frequency. With these conditions in mind, it is possible to suggest that the intensifying levels of commodification in the late capitalist period must be partnered by a growing emphasis on the visual. The strength of the relationship between the act of looking and the act of consuming means that if consumerism increases then that increase must be both shadowed by and, to an extent, dependent upon a concomitant growth in the significance of the act of looking. The 'frenzy of the visible' can thus be tied to the frenzy of late capitalist consumerism.[21] This sense of the links that bind the commodity to the visual is, of course, central to the analysis of contemporary conditions developed by commentators like Guy Debord. For Debord economics meets the visual in the society of the spectacle, a frozen life world of objects that are made to be seen and consumed simultaneously. Debord offers a vision of a world that has 'been turned into a gigantic spectacle in which the visible form of the commodity totally occup[ies] everyday life, uniting production and consumption in one monstrous system'.[22] The capitalist spectacle creates conditions in which the 'totality of the commodity world is visible in one piece'.[23]

Debord's insight into the relationship between the commercial and the visual provides crucial background for the

kinds of sexual spectacles offered by Susanna Moore. Having
identified the ways in which the sexual turn in recent culture
can be identified with the contemporary's emphasis on the
visual, Debord's reflections on the society of the spectacle
make it possible to go on and identify that visual turn with
contemporary capitalist structures. The result is a sense of the
ways in which the sexual, the visual and the economic all
intersect. This intersection is important because it offers a
way of establishing an explanatory perspective on the
emphatically sexualised dimensions in contemporary culture.
Instead of reading these elements in straightforward terms as
a product of the commercial logic that 'sex sells', they can be
interpreted, more specifically, as a manifestation of the
heightened emphasis on the visual in late twentieth-century
society and, on a wider level, as an expression of the intensified
levels of commodification generated by late capitalism.

These perspectives on the relationship between commodification and the representations of sex can be extended by
developing this reading of graphic sexual descriptions in blank
fiction to include a brief analysis of Richard Hell's *Go Now*
(1996). In *Go Now*, Richard Hell, former punk innovator with
the New York band Television, tells the story of Billy Mudd,
a failing musician caught in a drug-fuelled decline. The novel
follows Mudd's car journey across the American continent, a
trip that leads him through a series of intense sexual and
drug-related experiences. The narrative culminates in a meeting
between Mudd and his aunt, an encounter that leads inevitably
towards sex. This graphic scene reaches its conclusion when
Mudd's orgasm is interrupted by the sight of Chrissa, his
travelling companion and former girlfriend, standing at the
foot of the bed with a camera in her hand. Hell writes:

[Chrissa] has a camera to her eye and has started clicking
off flash pictures ... Camera flashes popping off capture my
aunt's unbearable confusion and horror as she finally sees
Chrissa and jolts and screams. I am crouched up like a
preying monkey behind and above her, frozen but gorged
with adrenalin.[24]

In this sequence Mudd's sexual encounter is concluded in terms that offer a strong sense of the primacy of the visual. Not only is the liaison with his aunt depicted in predictably graphic, or perhaps even cinematographic, terms, but the moment of orgasm is seen through Chrissa's lens. The camera passes its masterful eye over the scene and, in a way that fits neatly with the camera's mythical role as the stealer of souls, produces a reified image of the events. The use of words like 'capture' and 'frozen' makes this reification explicit. Thus, like *In the Cut, Go Now* establishes a clear equation between the sexual act and the act of looking.

Despite the existence of this relationship, a wider sense of the way in which the events described in this scene can be tied to the economic seems elusive. An image of commodification can be found in Hell's depiction of the reifying effects of the camera. Similarly, the presence of the camera seems to turn Mudd's activities into a sexual spectacle. The problem is that neither of these points provide a really concrete link between this description and the economic. It is possible, however, to identify such a connection by looking at the way in which this scene depicts the moment of orgasm and linking that depiction with a terminology filtered from commercial pornography. As Linda Williams explains, 'the industry's slang term for the moment the hard-core film "delivers the goods" of sexual pleasure ... [is] the money shot'.[25] In *Go Now*, Mudd's 'money' is spent at the point of orgasm, a moment that coincides with the popping of the flash and the movement of the shutter. The act of spending is thus dramatised in a sequence that seems, in its relationship to the pornographer's 'money shot', to offer 'the perfect embodiment of the illusory and insubstantial ... "society of the spectacle" of advanced capitalism.'[26] This scene thus links money to the visual and the sexual. The moment of orgasm is the moment in which sex is transformed into a commodity, frozen both visually by the camera lens and, in the act of exchanging and spending bodily fluids, economically. In this way Hell's writing, like Moore's, represents the intersection of the sexual, the visual and the economic.

Like Moore and Hell, the work of African-American writer Sapphire engages with a similar range of concerns. Her writing establishes a crucial awareness of the relationship between sex and the spectacle and offers images that reflect those developed in *Go Now* and *In the Cut*. In her collection of blank stories and fragmented poems, *American Dreams* (1994), Sapphire offers a piece called 'Trilogy', a narrative that provides a series of glimpses into the life of a stripper. In one section the narrator describes

> The men in the booths, the freaks, I watched them drop quarters, crook their fingers, beckon, unzip their pants ... OOHH they would go as they begged us to look, as if it was good. We laughed at them as they looked at us. They jacked off, rolling their eyes, shaking, pissing in the booths. Rasta men, Hasidic Jews, Asian businessmen, slick young-looking niggers, bowing before a need in the booth. We needed the money.[27]

Here, once again, the stress is on the connections between the commercial, the sexual and the visual. The viewers are seen dropping their quarters and rolling their eyes, an indignity that is endured because the women need 'the money'. The masterful commercial eye consumes their bodies, looking, positioning, freezing and controlling.

As was the case with *In the Cut* and *Go Now*, Sapphire's 'Trilogy' offers a vision of a world in which the representations of graphic sexual spectacles become scenes that merge the visual and the commercial. The objectified representations of sexuality offered in these three pieces are thus regarded as elements that thematise the impact of commodification. In these texts sex becomes a spectacle, a process that seems to speak of a world in which capitalism's incorporating, colonising and commodifying power is intensifying.

This analysis of the ways in which these sexual images can be regarded as commodities, and identified as integrated parts of the late capitalist spectacle, offers a vision of a world in which all aspects of human life have been colonised by contemporary economic structures. It seems that this system is capable of commodifying anything and everything. In the same way that the previous chapter linked violence to commodification, this discussion makes a connection between the sexual turn and the intensifying commercial processes of late twentieth-century capitalism. The vision offered is a gloomy one. Contemporary culture is dominated by commodification, a process which leads, it seems, to freezing, objectification and in many cases death. This negative view needs, however, to be balanced against a sense of the ways in which these texts articulate elements that appear to resist or refuse total incorporation. Commodification, these novels suggest, doesn't always lead to stultification.

Resistance to these deadening effects is expressed, in simple terms, through the emphasis both *In the Cut* and *Go Now* place on sexual pleasure. Neither Susanna Moore's Frannie nor Richard Hell's Mudd allow their senses to be completely deadened by the reifications they experience. On the contrary, both characters experience profound erotic sensations, feelings that emerge, paradoxically, during the process of objectification. When, for example, Mudd observes Chrissa freezing his image, this observation seems to heighten his sexual arousal rather than deaden it. Mudd is both 'frozen' and 'gorged with adrenalin'. Similarly Frannie, despite undergoing a series of objectifying experiences, finds herself moving towards ever more extreme states of sexual arousal. It thus appears that both novels balance their images of frozen, commodified sexuality with a sense of the ways in which the erotic can be seen to liberate, albeit momentarily. Late capitalism, it seems, is unable to fully incorporate eroticism.

This perspective on the erotic can be deepened by looking at the work of Georges Bataille. For Bataille the 'erotic is fundamentally transgressive of taboos and limitations'.[28] Central to this transgression is the challenge the erotic offers to 'the primacy of sight'.[29] The suggestion is that Bataille's representations of eroticism engage authority through mechanisms aimed at 'the dethronement of the eye', processes that are dramatised in Bataille's most famous piece *The Story of the Eye* (1928).[30] As Roland Barthes observes, *The Story of the Eye* revolves around a semiological puzzle generated by the aural and symbolic relations that develop between '*oiel*', '*oeuf*', '*soleil*' and '*couille*'.[31] The connections Bataille establishes link the eye to the egg, to the sun, to the testicle and, by association, to excrement and the anus. These linkages inevitably problematise the power of the visual. For Bataille erotic experience involves a need to go beyond the limits of the known. To move beyond the known it is necessary to move out of sight, a movement that is facilitated by these relentless attempts to offend the eye. It is this process of eroding and exceeding the power of sight that thus becomes central to Bataille's conception of the erotic. Bataille's work insists on the connection between the erotic's transgressive power and the attempt to exceed or undermine the authority of the visual.

The emphasis on the visual can be connected to Bataille's stress on the role of excess in his explorations of eroticism. In Bataille's work the indulgent extremes reached in the pursuit of erotic experiences involve a search for excesses that lead ultimately to transgression. This discussion of the ways in which the erotic depends upon the production of excesses gestures towards the existence of an erotic economy in which 'gratuitous expenditure' plays a crucial role.[32] This excessive economy is obviously inimical to regulation of any kind. The diverse and indulgent experiences of the erotic combine 'heterogeneous existence' with 'unproductive expenditure' in an arrangement that is 'irreducibly ambiguous'.[33] The result is a system that exceeds all boundaries by generating extreme, superfluous experiences. The challenge to order posed by excess is thus seen to destabilise regulating forces and, in particular, to challenge ordered systems of exchange. This sense of the transgressive role played by excess can be connected with an understanding of the way in which Bataille's writing works to undermine the authority of the visual to produce a general perspective on the ways in which both eroticism and excess might problematise the perceived stability of the sexual spectacle. In denigrating the power of the visual and the forces of regulation, excessive eroticism refuses integration. Where, in previous parts of this discussion, the relationships that connected sex and the spectacle seemed to underline the dominance of capitalist forces, Bataille's work introduces a sense of the instability of this network of forces. Erotic spectacles of sexual excess thus become both emblems of late capitalism's commodifying power and, simultaneously, elements that generate energies that are in fact hostile to that power. In colonising the erotic, capitalism incorporates forces that are ultimately unproductive.

This brief reading of Bataille's understanding of the deregulating influence of eroticism and excess can, through this emphasis on sex and the spectacle, be connected to the specific ideas being discussed here and is particularly interesting because it raises the possibility of reading these blank fictions in terms that recognise the destabilising forces lying within their representations of sexual spectacles. A brief reflection on the opportunities that exist for linking these ideas to the graphic sexual imagery in Sapphire's 'Trilogy' provides a perspective on this position.

While on one level 'Trilogy' can be seen to represent the objectifications of the female body by a commercially motivated male gaze, there is another sense in which this text produces an image of the ways in which that process of objectification is destabilised. When the men stare at the women in the booths, Sapphire describes them 'bowing before the need', a situation that weakens their assumed control. The mastery of the commercial eye is disturbed, the women get the money and seem, in some respects, to enslave the men around them. The commercial spectacle of the striptease creates energies that problematise the assumed mastery of both sight and capital. Thus Sapphire offers a narrative in which the erotic disturbs the putative integration of the sexual spectacle. The search for a reified sexual image leads to a confrontation with an excessive eroticism that weakens the authority of the commodifying impulse.

This focus on the erotic excesses in 'Trilogy' can be connected to the work of a writer for whom these ideas provide one of the principal foci. Though clear echoes of Bataille's work can be found in the writing of Sapphire, Moore and Hell, nowhere, it seems, is Bataille's legacy more valued than it is in the work of Dennis Cooper. In *Frisk*, for example, it is the conjunction of brutalising sex with the objectifications of murder that provides the basis for the narrative, an intersection that owes an obvious debt to Bataille. The influence of Bataille, clearly visible in *Frisk*, is also readily apparent in Cooper's most recent novel *Try* (1994).

Set against Cooper's favourite Californian backdrop, *Try* offers a portrait of the tangled network of relationships that develop among a group of young and not-so-young gay men. In one narrative strand, Cooper describes the seduction and corruption of the adolescent Robin by the older Ken, an individual who is willing to use money, drugs and coercion in the pursuit of his sexual desires. This sequence includes the following scene:

> 'Let's make that video,' Ken said. He could taste Robin's shit kind of generally. 'Up, up,' he added, and slapped the flushed butt.
> Robin tottered into another room.
> Light.
> 'Wow.' The kid gasped, hid his eyes. 'Man that's intense.' He could see a camera. The motel-looking bed. Ken way off to the left, naked, fat. 'But ... I don't know,' he added.
> 'All right *three* hundred dollars.'[34]

Like Bataille's *oeill, oeuf, soleil, couille*, Cooper offers a description in which an associative relationship is established between excrement, money, the eye, the anus and the camera lens. What makes these allusions interesting is not only that they seem to reflect the kinds of ideas developed in *The Story of the Eye*, but also that they can be fitted in alongside this discussion's general sense of the links that bind the visual, the sexual and the economic. The kid's appearance in the video is dependent on a commercial bargain, the '*three* hundred dollars'. Cooper strengthens this impression by showing Ken's thought processes move from 'the video' to 'shit'. The association between the eye, excrement and money not only echoes the kind of excremental bargains forged in Cooper's *Frisk*, but also identifies the visual as a mortifying agent. This pattern of relationships establishes a negative perspective on both the act of looking and also, though less obviously, the deadening effects of the economic. The kid hides his eyes, unwilling to contemplate the impending degradation, an imaginative flight that signals a wider anxiety about his participation in the production of this sexual spectacle.

This chapter began with the suggestion that the prevalence of explicit sexual imagery in contemporary culture needed some kind of explanation. In the course of this discussion, a connection has been established between the graphic images offered in recent American fiction and wider conditions established by contemporary capitalism. Like violence, it is the relationship with late capitalism that has made these representations intelligible. The crucial point is that though sex seems to have been identified with the increasingly powerful processes of commodification, lying within these representations is a sense that these integrating mechanisms contain contrary energies. Excessive eroticism seems to signal both an expansion of the reified sphere while at the same time marking the weakening of that sphere. The sexual spectacle exceeds regulation. In this respect the focus on objectified sexuality doesn't necessarily produce an image of a totally reified world.

4

Shopping

Reflection on the relationships between commodification and the representations of violence and explicit sexuality in blank fiction has produced a powerful image of the extent to which late twentieth-century experiences have become integrated into the commercialised world of late capitalism. The course of this discussion has, however, uncovered fleeting experiences that seem able to live and grow on this apparently dead terrain. While it is possible to encounter glimpses of these dynamics in the spectacular corpse-strewn narratives of Moore, Cooper and Ellis, a much more clearly defined image can be developed by looking at the work of Lynne Tillman.

Though primarily a novelist, Tillman's association with a variety of universities and her interest in academic thinking mark her as a self-consciously intellectual writer. Her co-editorship of *Beyond Recognition*, a collection of essays by Craig Owens, shows the range of her interests and typifies the work of an individual who feels comfortable moving between the critical and the creative.[1] Her position is bolstered by her wide knowledge of the New York scene, her links with Warhol and the Factory and a creative output that includes three novels, a large number of short stories and work on the film *Committed* (1984). Her intellectualism and artistic range is reflected in the quiet, thoughtful tone of her fiction and her focus on the internal life of her characters. This approach has meant that Tillman's work has neither received as much attention as the more explicit writing of her contemporaries nor been confronted with the charges of sensationalism that have closed around these more dramatic narratives. In this sense her work can be differentiated from that of Moore, Ellis and Cooper. There are however similarities for, despite its thoughtful mood, Tillman's fiction has not avoided the allegations of weightlessness and emptiness that seem to typify critical responses to blank fictions. In one representative commentary, Brian Wallis suggests that the characters in Tillman's novels

> move with a sense of somnolence, drifting through their lives with a seeming distance and dispassion. The formal structure of the writing emphasizes the lack of wilfulness through a curious stream-of-consciousness which moves the narrative through a series of displacements ... these little jumps ... do not take place through time. Instead they are prompted by linguistic association ... random formations of abstractly linked words determine behaviour.[2]

With the emphasis on abstractions, 'random formations' and the somnolent drifting mood, Wallis offers a portrait of a blank fiction divorced from wider material realities.

This position does not, however, square with Tillman's conception of her own work. She is concerned that

> the country is falling apart, what does anything matter, people are dying, starving ... and what does anything matter, what difference does this make, what matter do words make?[3]

Here she rejects abstraction, developing a social conscience and concerning herself with the relationship between literature and context. Her stated intention is to question the apparently referent-free logic of contemporary culture and to produce texts that bridge the gap between the linguistic and the material. The consequence is that there appears to be a conflict between the looseness of Tillman's fictions and her desire to produce texts that disclose the 'matter' around which their aesthetic forms are built. It is this tension between blank weightlessness and a concern for the social and the material that provides Tillman's work with one of its most potent dynamics, an energy that can be understood in clearer terms by looking at 'Weird fucks', a story from her collection *Absence Makes the Heart* (1990).

The descriptions of casual sex and fleeting encounters offered in 'Weird fucks' seem to provide ideal thematic partners for Tillman's apparently loose, abstract aesthetic. In a narrative that follows a path as aimless and slippery as the structure of the text itself, the story describes a journey across America and Europe as the narrator wanders in and out of countries, jobs and relationships. Her sexual encounters take her from Maine to New York to London to Amsterdam and beyond in a journey that has as much to do with her quest for sexual experiences and personal identity as it does with travelling. With this journey Tillman finds an image for rootless and emotional blankness. Her narrator seems content to drift through life, indifferent and untouched by the world outside.

This impression is disturbed, however, by moments in the text that appear to break through this glassy surface and provide a detailed insight into the ways in which this loose collection of events are tied to much more profound experiences. This process is articulated in the narrative's concluding section, a paragraph in which the narrator reflects on a failed relationship and observes that

> He hadn't been a one night stand, a temporary shelter like a glassed-in bus stop on a busy rainy street ... He had attenuated the one-night stand into something more difficult to get over. For a while I was meaner in the clinches, not so easy to fool.[4]

The temporary nature of the one night stand is contrasted against the narrator's enduring bitterness. She is unable to 'forgive' and 'not so easy to fool', a determination that cuts against the *laissez faire* attitudes exhibited in other parts of the story. With these emotions pushed to the fore, it becomes possible to interpret this section as a moment in which the text reveals the depth of feeling that has underpinned many of the narrator's actions. The extent of her emotions are, as the key phrase in this section makes clear, 'difficult to get over'. The awkward process of revelation, set in motion by this failed relationship, has left her confronting an uneasy skeleton of experiences that she is unable either to bury or to forget. This attenuation, this abstracting, minimalising process, creates the conditions in which the realities of her emotional situation are brought to the fore, a dynamic that introduces substance into the apparently empty text.

These elements not only add to the understanding of the narrator's experiences but also offer insights into the dynamics of the text itself, hinting that it, like the narrator, discovers depth and significance in the casual movements of its 'attenuated' form. Like a one night stand, the narrative seems as flimsy and insubstantial as the 'temporary shelter' afforded by a 'glassed-in bus stop', but this transparency belies more substantial dimensions. These dimensions are apparent throughout the text and emerge clearly in a section that describes an idyllic English summer:

> We went to his cottage in Norfolk, listened to Stevie Wonder on the radio and I wrote letters about cricket, actors, country life; my letters were shaped with Jane Austen in mind ... We visited the neighbouring lord and had a discussion about tied cottages. The pound may have dropped as we spoke.[5]

In these lines Tillman paints in typically broad strokes. First impressions suggest that this passage performs a simple descriptive function. She lists the events without elaborating upon them and employs a simple unadorned language. The meanings contained within the passage seem self-explanatory. This impression is, however, misleading. Tillman's writing might appear light and superficial, but deeper concerns lie just below the surface. These issues emerge in the account of the couple's visit to the 'neighbouring lord and [their] ... discussion about tied cottages'. Here the narrator's observations are given an obviously economic resonance, dimensions that alert the reader to the realities upon which this rural idyll depends. In the portrait of the lord we are offered an image of the landowner engaged in a discussion about tenancy arrangements. Ending the paragraph with the words 'the pound may have dropped as we spoke' only serves to emphasise these elements and to ground the whole description in these specific material conditions.

The abstract tone and meditative atmosphere that characterises Tillman's writing thus seems, in this story at least, to belie an emphasis on the weighty and the material. The blankness of her fiction is not a function of an aimless literary project but works alongside this concern for context.

It is the contrast between the heavy and light that gives these passages their energy. The fact that Tillman introduces these elements through an emphasis on an economic dimension is of particular relevance to this discussion. In this section she grounds the experiences described in 'Weird fucks' on commercial realities. This is significant because it both connects her work to the ideas generated in the analysis of representations of violence and extreme sexuality and also provides a way of interrogating arguments that conceive Tillman as a writer absorbed in familiar reflections on subjectivity and inspired by 'the usual postmodern suspicions about the trickery of fictional processes'.[6] This focus on the material dimensions of the experiences she describes complicates the portrait of Tillman as a postmodernist. Her writing, though engaged in abstract semiological processes, combines those trajectories with a focus on material concerns that disrupt the free-floating self-reflexivity of her apparent postmodernism. The importance of these elements in Tillman's work can be underlined by looking beyond the directions taken in 'Weird fucks' and considering the dynamics of *Motion Sickness* (1991), a novel that develops many of the concerns established in her earlier work to produce a text in which the tensions between abstraction and contextualisation play a central role.

In *Motion Sickness*, Tillman offers an account of a nameless American woman's wanderings across Europe and North Africa. In a novel that echoes the kinds of ideas developed in 'Weird fucks', Tillman's narrator criss-crosses the 'old' world, self-consciously meditating on the significance of these environments and, more importantly, her relationship with them. The narrative's account of her journey from place to place is paralleled by its descriptions of her emotional voyage and her encounters with a wide variety of different people. Not only does she move from one country to the next, but she also slips easily outside the borders of one casual friendship and on to the territory of another. The reader witnesses her dealings with the shady Sal, her love affair with Zoran, the Yugoslav, her relationship with the English brothers Paul and Alfred and her involvement in the marriage between Jessica, the American expatriate, and Charles, her unreliable English husband. The narrative's mixing of people and places is mirrored in the structure of the text which, using associative links to connect the sequences together rather than a straightforward chronology, moves in a typically drifting, associative fashion. The novel's loose, overlapping movements seem to reinforce the impression that the narrator's journey is casual and directionless. The overall feeling is that it is the narrator's imagination that provides the text with its most important terrain, a space in which character, time and place all seem to mix and merge. Even at the novel's end little seems to have been concluded. Jessica and Charles may have effected a reunion, but the narrator herself still appears to be unsure as to her next move. The suspicion is that she is preparing to go back to New York, but the novel ends without disclosing her final destination. Inevitably, her journey has been one in which the discoveries of travel have outweighed the revelations of arrival.

Throughout the course of this narrative Tillman constructs a dialogue between her narrator's situation and traditional American concerns about the relationship between Europe and the 'new' world. These issues are brought to the fore in Tillman's emphasis on her narrator's reading habits and her constant allusions to literary characters like Henry James's Isabel Archer and Graham Greene's Alden Pyle who seem to represent this confrontation between Europe and America.[7] These ideas are strengthened by the narrator's anxieties about her own identity and her self-conscious attempts to explore what it means to be an American in Europe. In one characteristic sequence she finds herself staring into 'the mirror over the hotel dresser' and observing that this reflected image 'offers no relief, no clue to my larger role in the larger story, one that is not easily framed and can't be studied objectively, can't take the country out of the girl when the girl is out of the country'.[8] The implication is that the ambiguous position of the American woman in Europe must remain unresolved. It is something that is too complex to be 'easily framed', too unstable to be 'studied objectively'. She is left pondering the relationship between 'the girl' and 'the country', and reflecting on the unquestionable, though indefinable, influence of her origins.

These anxieties seem to underpin many of the narrator's thoughts and provide the impulse behind both her intellectual doubts and her geographical wanderings. Despite the sense of insecurity these kinds of thoughts reveal, there is a feeling that the narrator does, to an extent, welcome the invisibility her displaced status brings. At times she celebrates her role, saying 'I am drifting, *derivé*, nearly anonymous, and in a state of mind conducive to corners and walls, where I stand alone, almost happy for the way I can spy and won't be seen, will remain unrecognised'.[9] This sense of voyeurism is crucial to the direction of the text, allowing her to drift free from the structures that control the people around her and to continue her freewheeling exploration of cultures, identities and experiences. It is her 'motion sickness', the desire to keep herself in motion, that propels the narrative and gives the narrator the kind of distance she requires. This search for a position from which she can 'spy' without being seen is not, however, as the title of the novel suggests, without its drawbacks. Though free to indulge her yearning for mobility, that motion also makes her sick, an illness that is caused both by her own movement and the eternal motion she sees around her.

With this range of concerns established at the heart of the novel, *Motion Sickness* develops into a narrative in which questions linked to subjectivity become crucial. The result is a complex work in which the path of one fluid, mobile figure is plotted against a background that is itself equally transient. Unravelling the novel's structural, thematic and stylistic threads is, as a result, difficult. It is possible, however, to develop a more concrete perspective on these elements by looking at the way Tillman connects fluid fictional patterns to the specifics of context and, more particularly, to the material realities of the economic sphere. Representations of tourism and consumerism provide the novel with some of its central images and offer both an insight into the text itself and an opportunity for developing this discussion's reflections on the relationship between blank fictions and contemporary capitalism.

Throughout the novel Tillman's narrator seems semi-consciously aware of the connections between the motion sickness she feels and the kinds of conditions created by late capitalism. At one point, following a series of political discussions with her lover, she concludes that 'I can feel entirely indifferent to the content of what I say. A great postindustrial ennui sweeps away vestiges of involvement'.[10] Where other parts of the text suggest that her state of mind is a product of either her nationality or her restlessness, here her 'ennui' is tied much more specifically to contemporary economics. It is this force, she feels, that has swept away the last 'vestiges of involvement'. These concerns are developed further in the narrative's focus on that most classically postindustrial enterprise, tourism.

The novel's emphasis on sites of 'historical significance', foreign cultures and exotic locations offers a ready image of the eclecticism and semiotic abstraction that many commentators identify as characteristic of postmodern culture. In *The Tourist Gaze*, John Urry argues that the tourist's attention is drawn towards 'features of landscape and townscape which separate them off from everyday experience ... the gaze is constructed through signs and tourism involves the collection of signs'.[11] This process is dramatised in Tillman's description of her narrator's collection of postcards. 'From the postcards I buy', she writes, 'I know what churches and galleries I ought to visit.'[12] It is the image that has become more important to her than the reality of the visit, an image that she can acquire, keep and organise in her own private simulation of the world. When, at the end of the novel, she scatters these postcards across the bed of her hotel room, she forms the collection of images into a collage-like representation of her travels. Like the act of sightseeing itself, these pictures produce a composite visual representation of a world that has been separated off from the specifics of time and space by the tourist gaze.

Though Tillman's narrator seems to create an abstract world in her free-floating imagination, the novel makes it clear that her experiences are founded on particular kinds of material relations. In one exemplary section the narrator's thought process begins with a reflection on the currencies of different countries. She describes how, after changing her money, she receives 'large colourful notes for smaller English ones' then immediately uses these new notes to 'buy black-and-white real-photo postcards of places I haven't visited'.[13] The jump from currency to postcards suggests that both the notes and the cards are in some way emblematic of her status as a tourist. They represent her journey, speaking simultaneously of the places she has been (or not as is the case in this instance) and also of the money that she has spent. This process of delineating the commercial dimensions of the narrator's journey is developed in the description of her visit to Venice and her account of 'another visitor [who] makes her presence felt by moving from alcove to alcove and dropping fifty lire in slots in metal boxes which activate spotlights. Sudden illuminations fiercely disrupt the quiet dark spaces.'[14] The portrait of this woman bringing the secular light of the fifty lire piece into the interior of the church offers a graphic image of the links between commerce and the tourist gaze. The fact that money brings illumination gestures both towards a sense of the commodification of this particular kind of cultural experience and, more significantly perhaps, provides further insight into the narrative's sensitivity to the commercial influences that underpin the events it describes.

Thus, through the inclusion of these detailed descriptions of moments in her narrator's journey, Tillman offers a repeated emphasis on the economics of travelling. These meditations shadow the kinds of observations John Urry makes about tourism in *The End of Organized Capitalism*, where, with Scott Lash, he concludes that tourism is linked to 'cultural fragmentation and pluralism ... [and] the commodification of leisure'.[15] Their thesis has obvious links to Mandel's appreciation of the fact that late capitalism is a period in which 'recreation' is becoming just as involved in the 'sphere of production ... as the organization of work'.[16] The position is that this kind of contemporary cultural practice is grounded on new geographical, social and, in particular, economic conditions. As Urry argues, the kind of flexible, independently organised travelling of the type described in *Motion Sickness* is characteristic of late capitalism.[17] In this respect, the free-floating journeys depicted in *Motion Sickness* need not be interpreted as a reflection on postmodern culture, nor regarded as a postmodernist meditation on identity and subjectivity, but can be read, instead, as events that position these postmodernist elements firmly within the context of late capitalism. The suggestion is that *Motion Sickness*'s constant focus on the economic sphere makes it a novel in which postmodernism is seen in terms of the material conditions of contemporary society.

It is through the emphasis on economics and, in particular, the concern for the casual details of contemporary consumerism that Tillman develops this relationship between the aesthetic and philosophical terrains of the postmodernist imagination and the concrete concerns of late capitalism. On a very basic level, a novel that includes chapters entitled 'Tourist attractions', 'Small pleasures' and 'Indulgences' shows itself to be very obviously engaged in the processes and practices of consuming. The implication is that *Motion Sickness* is a novel in which the relationships between aesthetics and cultural context are being constantly surveyed. This suggestion can be tied more precisely to the specifics of the text by looking at the detailed emphasis Tillman places on acts of consumption.

Throughout the novel the narrator haunts shops, cafes, tourist traps and market places. The experiential events in her journey are thus given an obviously economic edge and her reflections on her internal reality are seen to hinge as much upon what she has bought as they do upon what she has seen and where she has been. This exploration can be illustrated by examining a section in which the narrator finds herself sitting outside a hotel in Tangier and observing the city in terms that blend the semiotic eclecticism of the tourist gaze with a subtle recognition of the inescapably material foundations upon which that gaze depends. Tillman writes:

The hotel patio overlooks the Socco, offering, as in the tourist brochure, a panoramic view of the city. With binoculars I could watch individual men opening their small stores, see their expressions, and follow women in the crowded markets at the bottom of the road, and see the intensity of their lives at a distance. I once read that safety is an acceptable level of risk. The patio is always hard to leave. It was hard to leave Pete though I'll see him later. This

room is difficult to leave. I like it with its window on the
world. I like windows. Windows of opportunity.[18]

In this description, like the true tourist, the narrator takes the
role of the outsider. She is, in her own figuration, blankly
staring at the scene in front of her, cut off from the life of the
city, watching it, or imagining herself watching it, through
binoculars. Her sense of distance and disinterested voyeurism
are, however, illusions. She is staying in a hotel and obviously
paying the bill. Her imaginary reflections on the people
shopping in the market can, in this context, be regarded as an
acknowledgement of the economic foundations upon which
her illusions rest. In her daydream she creates a scenario in
which she imagines people buying food for the hotel with her
money. Despite her assumed detachment, she thus reveals the
fact that she is unable to cut herself off from the material
realities of the world outside.

The specific details offered in this section strengthen the
sense of the importance of the economic. On a superficial level,
her observations appear to spill out onto the page in a random
manner, a pattern that seems to constitute an attempt to
recreate the episodic organisation of the daydream. Some of
her thoughts look incongruous ('safety is an acceptable level
of risk'), while others appear almost dreamlike ('the intensity
of their lives at a distance'). The overall feeling is that this
section provides a carefully unstructured insight into the
sketchy processes of the narrator's mind. These random
impressions need, however, to be balanced against an
understanding of the ways in which her thoughts are tied to
a view of the market. Not only do these thoughts carry her from
the economically defined tourist environment of the hotel into
a fantasy about 'individual men opening their small stores' and
on beyond that to the entrepreneurial thought 'I like windows.
Windows of opportunity', but both the language of the piece
and its imagery seem coloured by economic tones. In her
clichéd reference to the 'panoramic view of the city' lies an
echo of the 'tourist brochure'. More revealing still is the fact
that this cliché is focused around the consumerist desire
represented by the binoculars, an object that, if acquired,
would enable her to see things that, at present, she can only

imagine. In a thought process that mimics the movements of an advertising campaign, she finds herself equating ownership with power and comes to regard the binoculars as an object that would both literally and metaphorically improve her view of the world.[19]

The scene she describes is thus presented in a way that insists on the purchasing of a product that would transform the conditional phrase 'I could watch' into a reality. The tourist gaze's commodifying power finds, as a result, a physical form in a sequence in which that gaze is seen to be itself dependent upon a commodity. Tillman's consciousness of the manner in which commercial forces underpin her narrator's experience discovers a concrete expression in the image of the Socco. Abstract economic mechanisms are thus given physical dimensions in a scene that links them to the precise geographical space from which the financial metaphors of market and exchange are derived.

These processes echo the dynamics of an earlier scene in which the narrator describes a day spent shopping for vegetables in London:

> Walking on Queensway I'm carrying a container of humus and a bag of tomatoes. I like the way they sell tomatoes here: hard ripe English tomatoes. Hand-lettered signs or shouts from the people hawking them. On Portobello Road women and men with bright red swollen hands hold the tomatoes above their heads or wave little paper bags and call you dear or luv.[20]

In this sequence Tillman's description of the street vendors selling 'hard ripe English tomatoes' is offered in terms that place an emphasis on reification. Their hands, in terms that employ a kind of substitution, are seen to be 'bright red' and 'swollen', with the impression being that their bodies have been turned into commodities and become indistinguishable from their produce. This feeling is strengthened in the reference to the prices written on 'hand-lettered signs'. If, as this description suggests, the hands are subsumed by the product, then that product has, in a sense, been responsible for setting its own value. The hand of the worker is thus turned into the commodity, a transformation that speaks of the concealed, but nonetheless significant, effects of commodification. What makes this section interesting is that it connects the narrator's point of view with the processes of reification. As her language suggests, she seems to be experiencing the world in commodified terms, and is, temporarily at least, unable to differentiate between the people and the products. The employment of this reification can thus be connected to the novel's more general preoccupation with the commodified experiences of tourism. Not only does Tillman emphasise the consumerism that drives her narrator's journey, but she adds to that impression by employing, in this section at least, a narrative style that suggests that the narrator's vision is itself operating in a commodifying manner.

This emphasis on commodification inevitably establishes a link between this view of Tillman's writing and familiar accounts of the function of reification and its relationship with literature. In what is perhaps the most famous of these interpretations, Georg Lukács's essay 'Reification and the consciousness of the proletariat', Lukács offers a vision of reification's dehumanising effects:

> The quantification of objects, their subordination to abstract mental categories makes its appearance in the life of the worker immediately a process of abstraction of which he is the victim, and which cuts him off from his labour-power, forcing him to sell it on the market as a commodity, belonging to him. And by selling this, his only commodity, he integrates it (and himself: for his commodity is inseparable from his physical existence) into a specialised process that has been rationalized and mechanized, a process that he discovers already existing, complete and able to function without him and in which he is no more than a cipher reduced to an abstract quality, a mechanized and rationalized tool.[21]

In Lukács's reading, the worker is reification's 'victim', someone who has been transformed into a 'mechanized and rationalized tool.' The mechanisms of capitalism, so heavily tied to the commodity form, are thus seen to integrate the individual into a system that deadens and stultifies, a process that can only become more acute as capitalism develops and expands. This has specific implications for late capitalism: if dehumanisation is the consequence of the levels of commodification in the monopoly capitalist period discussed by Lukács, then this process must be even more severe in the late capitalist period, an age characterised by ever-increasing levels of commodification and economic penetration. It is this vision of a thoroughly integrated consumer society that provides a key strand in Fredric Jameson's reading of the 'logic of late capitalism' and forms the basis for his suggestion that the contemporary period is one in which a 'purer form' of capitalism has emerged, one that has an almost unimaginably complex, organised and impenetrable kind of authority.[22] In the late twentieth century, he argues,

> the socialization of labour is taken to its most extreme extent as the total accumulated result of the scientific and technical development of the whole society and humanity increasingly becomes the immediate precondition for each particular process of production in each sphere of production.[23]

In these terms, society seems closed and totalised. These processes are operating at an 'extreme extent' and signify the 'total accumulated' result of capitalist development in the contemporary period.

Jameson's conceptualisation of a contemporary society in which the individual is thoroughly integrated into a capitalist cycle echoes Theodore Adorno's and Max Horkheimer's influential reading of 'the culture industry as mass deception'. For them the consumer is frozen in the headlights of the on-rushing commercial machine and unable to act, think or move without its permission. Consumerism is the mark of this control for, in their terms, 'the triumph of advertising in the culture industry is that consumers feel compelled to buy and use its products, even though they see through them', a system that 'intentionally integrates its consumers from above'.[24] Like Adorno and Horkheimer, Jameson represents modern conditions in repressive terms. His argument is:

Postmodernism is the consumption of sheer commodification as process. The 'Life-style' of the superstate therefore
stands in relation to Marx's 'fetishism' of commodities as
the most advanced monotheisms to primitive animisms.[25]

In the late capitalist period, Jameson suggests, commercialisation has touched every kind of experiential sphere with the
implication being that this world is both totally fetishised
and fully integrated. There is no space beyond the
commodified terrains of the postmodern.

Jameson's totalised vision is not, however, reflected in
Tillman's *Motion Sickness*. Though it is a novel that represents
commodification's pervasive influence and dramatises the
extent to which commercial priorities regulate the narrator's
behaviour, there is no sense of her being totally controlled by
these late capitalist forces. Like Jameson, Tillman produces a
vision of a contemporary world in which commodification and
reification play a central role, but unlike him she does not see
this world as a place in which everything has been subsumed
to the logic of the late capitalist marketplace. The position she
adopts seems, instead, to shadow the kinds of arguments
proposed by Fred Pfeil, a commentator who rejects totalised
readings of contemporary culture as the 'inevitable extrusion
of an entire mode of production' in favour of an approach that
sees these formations as being part of a 'cultural aesthetic set
of pleasures and practices created by and for a particular social
group at a determinate moment in its collective history'.[26]
Pfeil's emphasis on culture's relationship with 'pleasures and
practices' seems particularly relevant to *Motion Sickness*, a
novel in which the narrator's individual gestures, enjoyments
and actions seem more important than any dominant
framework or logic. Though Pfeil's focus is on class where
Tillman's concern is for consumerism, both seem to share a
sense of the significance of individual practices. In these terms,
Motion Sickness can be interpreted as a novel that, in its attempt
to trace the implications raised by the 'pleasures and practices'
of consumerism and tourism, offers a way of thinking through
and beyond the kinds of rigid positions offered by a
commentator like Jameson. Tillman is concerned with the
commodity, but in her novel the commodity doesn't produce

an empty dehumanising experience. Instead consumerism becomes one of the mediums the protagonist uses to locate herself and communicate. Shopping, in these terms, becomes an imaginative, expressive exercise. She freewheels through the free market.

This suggestion provides a way of linking Tillman's aesthetic vision with a range of critical discourses that have emerged to question the kinds of totalised accounts of contemporary culture fostered by Jameson's reading of Mandel. In Douglas Kellner's and Stephen Best's terms, Jameson advances a 'monolithic model of postmodernism as a hegemonic form of contemporary culture' without saying exactly how the political and economic structure of late capitalism either produces or sustains such a hegemonic formation.[27] Even Mandel, the authority that provides the basis for Jameson's analysis of postmodernism, registers reservations about rigorously integrated visions, regarding them as a kind of 'neo-fatalist ideology'.[28] For him 'late capitalism is not a completely organised society at all. It is merely a hybrid, and bastardised *combination* of organisation and anarchy.'[29] The point is that late capitalism is a formation in which, despite its integrated appearance, contradictions and tensions still remain. The intensification of commercial activity does not inevitably lead to the production of a frozen, standardised world. Even Lukács appreciates the ways in which the reifying process produces contradictions. In his terms, it is possible 'to recognise the fetish character *of every commodity*', a recognition which empowers his critical project and encourages him to suggest ways of 'overcoming the contemplative standpoint of reification and ... "penetrating" its objects'.[30]

Tillman's emphasis on material conditions and the drifting consumerism of her narrator provide obvious links with the context of the late capitalist period. As these arguments suggest, however, there is no sense in which this connection signals a sense of passivity or subordination. Reification is a crucial force in the narrative, but it doesn't either dominate or deaden. Like those commentators who question totalised models of postmodernism and the culture of late capitalism, Tillman offers a vision of an individual wandering free through this endlessly commercial marketplace. Though her representations of consumerism function as images of the intensifying levels of commodification in the late capitalist period, the text does not offer a portrait of culture in which this commodification leads to total closure or restriction. On the contrary, it is in the very mechanisms of consumerism that Tillman's narrator finds her freedom, a process that might be paradoxical within the rigid, 'neo-fatalist' perspective offered by Jameson, but one that seems in tune with Mandel's sense of late capitalism as a 'bastardised *combination*'. As John Fiske argues, 'contemporary capitalist societies are too highly elaborated to be understood by a structural model'.[31] Commodification may provide one of the central structures for culture in the late twentieth century, but in terms of the arguments offered by commentators as diverse as Pfeil, Fiske and Mandel, it isn't a force that necessarily unites or homogenises experience. As the events in *Motion Sickness* suggest, commodification and the material conditions of late capitalism provide the central framework for existence, but this framework doesn't simply limit and control, it liberates as well.

These processes can be placed in clearer terms by looking more closely at the ways in which Tillman's novel dramatises the relationship between the economic and the personal. For Tillman the economic is part of her narrator's cultural experience. Her life, she feels,

> could be a fairy tale ... If it were a fairy tale there could be a reversal of fortune for me. Literal fortunes are reversed daily, as the dollar drops. Dutch paper money, ornate and florid, puts the American dollar in its place. The money has shrunk. Dollars look small and grim, worrying reminders of the American way. I have many more postcards than dollars, the postcards soothing to me as the shrunken dollars are to long-term foreign sufferers on Wall Street.[32]

Once again this description traces the material dimensions underpinning her tourist fantasies. In this passage she finds that, despite appearances to the contrary, she is not living in a fairy-tale. It is the currency of each country that seems to symbolise the material axis around which her experiences revolve. Tourism might appear to have released her into a free-floating space, but this is a 'fairy-tale', an illusion that depends upon her 'fortunes'. The narrator makes this clear when she describes how

> In a fairy tale I'd fall asleep and wake from this horrible dream of capture, a dream that seemed so real I could have sworn it had really happened. Some days pass like dreams, though one can imagine they really did happen. One day my money will run out, there won't be a pot of gold at the end of the rainbow ... My mother writes in her last letter, Someday you'll have to face the music.[33]

The economic imposes limits on her journey. She knows 'there won't be a pot of gold at the end of the rainbow' and that she will have to 'face the music'. She is sequestered within the boundaries defined by her economic situation, her life dependent upon the dynamics of her economic situation.

While the positions advanced in these sections seem to provide a fairly straightforward commentary on the financial foundations upon which all tourism depends, what makes Tillman's approach interesting is the way in which she represents her narrator's awareness of the economic boundaries that encircle her free-floating experiences in terms that seem to provide the narrator with ways of escaping those limitations. The sense of the determining power of material structures is, for example, undermined by the narrator's apparent indifference. Similarly, in the text's casual associative trajectories lies a formal image of the freewheeling journey described in the novel's content, a stylistic process that seems to reject closure or restriction. This loose style and her directionless, carefree journey challenge the simple mathematics of 'dollars', 'literal fortunes' and pots of gold. She appreciates the importance of financial concerns, but they do not completely dominate her behaviour. She is still able to dream and drift in her imagination, playing with these pecuniary imperatives without finding herself hopelessly caught up in them. She knows she can neither keep travelling forever nor elude commercial realities. She is able, however, for at least a little while longer, to keep dwelling in her fairy-tale existence.

The narrator's dream, a fantasy both in the literal sense and in the sense that tourism induces a kind of dream-like state, does not free her completely from the material realm. Instead it allows her to take up a position that is simultaneously inside and outside that realm. She is neither looking for a completely uncommodified experience, nor trying to find a privileged, utopian space to call her own. Instead, she simply recognises the limits while refusing to be completely bound by them. She knows what makes the world go round, but does not see these realities as the sum total of her experiences. She is a woman with 'more postcards than dollars' and though this is obviously a cause for concern, she manages to confront these nightmares with the knowledge that her postcards are as 'soothing to … [her] as the shrunken dollars are to long-term sufferers on Wall Street'. Thus, in her descriptions of these events, she makes it clear that while travel impoverishes her financially, it enriches her imaginatively, a process that enables her, at least temporarily, to transcend commercial constraints. She is able to drift along and enjoy the places where she can find brief liberation from economic determinism as she slides across the 'bastardized' structure of contemporary capitalism.

This thematic emphasis on the balance between freedom from and beholdenment to commercial imperatives is supported by formal elements in Tillman's text. Her conscious recognitions of reification and her efforts to peel away the crust of commodified culture and reveal the material relations lying beneath is facilitated by a narrative structure that seems to depend upon a loose dynamic that can be compared to the rolling interrogations of the narrative's content. In the passages discussed above there is evidence of the way Tillman's stylistic shifts enable her to move easily between different perspectives, positions that she links together in loose, associative strands. In the first section she jumps from fairy-tales to fortunes to detailed discussion of the appearance of a bank note and then on to 'Wall Street', while in the second she moves from dreams into 'a pot of gold' and then on to the letter from her mother. The associations spill out onto the page in a process that is not random but actually organised in a way that empowers the fiction's analysis of the relationship between the narrator's cultural experiences and her financial affairs. The different phrases and sentences are associated in terms that move away from meditations on imagination, cultural pleasure and sensory experience and on to reflections that are much more closely connected to economics. In the same way that the narrator's freewheeling journey brings her into conflict with the material realities that regulate her situation, the structure Tillman employs carries the text from the superficial to the profound in a journey that, smoothed by this narrative form, leads the reader towards a contemplation of these concealed material realities. The movements between the casual and the concrete that play such an important role in the novel's content are thus echoed in the formal dynamics of Tillman's writing.

Motion Sickness, in this way, offers a sense of the relationships that connect cultural experience to material context. Tillman's sensitivity to these relationships finds a more precise evocation in her narrator's reflections on the connections between language and commerce. These concerns come to the fore in a section that describes the narrator shopping in Amsterdam:

> In bread stores I ask for *bruin brood*, in cheese stores *oude kass* ... The storeowners hand me the goods and speak in English, as if somehow insulted that someone tried to speak their language ... If this is true, it could be because they're proud of their ability to speak many languages, or impatient with my lack of understanding of the hegemony of English, or it just takes less of their time to conduct business this way. The most routine transaction is cluttered with such considerations.[34]

In this description the search for the most economical communicative code leads the store-keepers to adopt English as the common linguistic denominator. The fact that their desire for an economical language is prompted in part by motivations that are themselves commercial adds an extra level to the narrator's meditations on international communication. It is obvious to her that 'it just takes less of their time to conduct business this way'. The communicative relationships developed are thus seen to depend as much on economics as they do on the use of English as a shared language. Commerce has enabled these conversations, a situation which suggests that a shared sense of economic priorities comes before a common cultural reference point.

The ideas generated in this scene are, of course, typical of the kinds of positions offered throughout *Motion Sickness*. What makes this sequence particularly interesting is the fact that it considers the links between language and commerce, relationships that are as important to the general communicative function of the text itself as they are to a woman trying to buy bread in a Dutch city. The suggestion is that these reflections on the narrator's specific linguistic situation be read as an exploration of the network of forces that link forms of expression with the material realm. There is even a sense in which Tillman might be considering the extent to which *Motion Sickness* as a whole, can be regarded as a novel in which, as the narrator suggests, 'the most routine transaction is cluttered with such considerations'. Tillman, in this section, thus seems determined to dramatise the relationship between language and economics, a desire that signals her wider grasp of the relationships that connect aesthetics to the material realm.

This network of forces is extended through the narrative's developing sense of the links that bind bodily pleasures to material realities. Like the work of Sapphire and Susanna Moore, Tillman sees a connection between sexuality and economics. Though their writing tends to deal with either violent or objectifying sexual experiences, Tillman shares their sense of the commercial nature of sexual encounters. In *Motion Sickness* the narrator feels liberated by travel and financial independence. She comments on 'the freedoms that money can buy' and observes that the act of 'buying a hotel room' is one in which she is 'psychologically unburdened' free to 'act out guilty pleasures, capitalist ones, no doubt'.[35] She imagines herself being unburdened psychologically and able to express herself, a liberation that comes through the economic. Hotel rooms are bought and the freedom given is marked both by guilt and the mercantile stamp of purchase.

The narrator's emphasis on the economics of pleasure develops throughout the course of her relationship with Zoran. Sex with him is akin to tourism, something she participates in and then moves on from. The casual consumerism of travel thus parallels her shifting sexual desires. This equation is established in a section that describes how

> We're best when we're in motion.
>
> Which is probably why we fuck most of the time. In this we've both become compulsive ... At a movie theatre he throws his coat over me ... We rush back to the guest house and fuck till we fall asleep. In the morning it begins again. Zoran is as good a lover as he was a sightseer in Venice.[36]

They are 'best' when they are in 'motion', a situation that underlines the parallel between tourism and their 'compulsive' sexuality. Zoran and Tillman's narrator consume sex in the same way that they consume the rest of the experiences around them. The suggestion that 'Zoran is as good a lover as he was a sightseer' makes this link explicit, a relationship that is strengthened in the passage's descriptions of their encounters in guest houses and cinemas. The implication is that not only do they 'fuck' in a way that shadows their sightseeing, they do so in the commercial spaces of movie theatres and, recalling the 'guilty', 'capitalist' pleasures described in earlier parts of the novel, rented rooms.

This sense of the forces that connect sexuality, economics and the narrator's own identity together is clarified in a section that describes her experiences in Amsterdam. Walking the streets she finds her attention drawn towards the prostitutes she sees around her. She wants to

> Look stealthily, secretly, at the prostitutes, who are not like Rembrandts, meant for abstract appreciation. I glance at them out of the corner of my eye, as if my look would be more fugitive than a man's – unwanted, not for profit, and robbing them somehow of what they are selling. Unless they are selling to women, which is something I haven't yet been able to discover. Probably not. And though some may be lesbians or bisexual, they may not have brought their predilections into the common marketplace.[37]

Once again the emphasis is on the 'common marketplace'. She is very aware that these women are not for 'abstract appreciation', but are selling themselves for obviously material purposes. Her thoughts, touched by a frisson of sexual desire, thus turn on a commercial axis. Prostitution is her focus, a profession that functions in this text, as it does in many blank fictions, as a symbol of the meeting of the economic and the erotic. In this scene the narrator attempts to 'get something for nothing', thus cheating the market. The sensual experience of looking allows her to transcend the marketplace for a moment. It is voyeurism that is free. She is observing women who have been transformed into commodities, but in that observation she is robbing them of what they are selling. Thus, even the image of the prostitute does not simply represent the total domination of the economic sphere.

It is the conflict between the narrator's loose reflections on sexuality and her awareness of commercial conditions that is dramatised in this scene, a tension that is left unresolved. Though conscious of the deadening impact of the market, she remains aware that, as she says in an earlier chapter, 'the social is definitely more than the sum of its parts'.[38] This awareness enables her to see, once again, beyond the limitations of the economic and to identify the uncommodified experiences that exist alongside and within the simple arithmetic of profit and loss.

As these elements show, *Motion Sickness* is a novel in which consumerism and economics play a central role. This engagement with late capitalism does not, however, mark it as a text that stands in the thrall of these economic processes. On the contrary, the text offers a vision of late capitalism's pervasive influence while simultaneously portraying an individual who lives and breathes in this environment. Her consumerism is not an index of her incorporation, but forms part of her negotiations with and around these material concerns. As Rob Shields argues, consumerism can be conceived as 'a form of social exchanges through which community influences and micro-powers are actualized'.[39] In an argument that rests heavily on Michel de Certeau's *The Practice of Everyday Life*, Shields interprets consumption as an act that allows the individual to construct an identity.

Unhappy with interpretations that read consumerism as mere subordination, these positions see consumption as an expressive act. They recognise the power and influence of commodification, but argue that consumers act from the bottom up as well as being acted upon from the top down.

These processes are relevant not only to *Motion Sickness*, but also to the rest of Tillman's fictions. Her narratives are, as Kasia Boddy observes, constantly attempting to 'examine the importance of cultural artefacts – books, paintings, films, TV programmes – in shaping as well as reflecting social conditions', a dynamic that identifies her work very strongly with the currents of mass culture.[40] *Motion Sickness*'s broad range of references to films, books and music is echoed in a story like 'Other movies' (1990), a piece in which almost all of the references and descriptions echo the scenes and styles of particular films. Similarly, Tillman's novel *Cast in Doubt* (1992) focuses on the tension between 'high' and 'low' culture as Horace, the narrator, struggles to balance his financial commitments to produce detective fiction against a desire to write a 'great work' of literature. In these texts Tillman's engagement with mass culture functions, like the consumerism described in *Motion Sickness*, as an index of the complexity of the position she adopts, a process that is, as the subsequent chapter will suggest, typical of other blank fictions.

This range of arguments offers a counter to the perspective that links Tillman's work to the terms of the postmodernist aesthetic. When, for example, Elizabeth Young argues that Tillman refuses to allow her narrator in *Motion Sickness*

> to establish 'communication' in sending her postcards ... they are 'postcards from the imaginary into the impossible real.' The postmodern novel is self-referential; its characters cannot 'communicate' with one another. They do not need to – they do not 'exist' and there is no plot.[41]

By identifying Tillman with a weightless postmodernism, she fails to grasp Tillman's sensitivity to context and her concern for the 'matter words make'. Her weightlessness is not an index of absence, but a force that actually helps her engage with material processes and find a space for 'communication' in the postmodern world.

In *Motion Sickness*, 'Weird fucks' and her other narratives, Tillman's writing displays the capacity to skirt around and skim over the everyday in ways that develop complex patterns of imaginative relationships between the experiences she describes and the wider context of the contemporary period. She neither locks herself into a fixed frame and tries to describe these conditions from the inside, nor stands apart from them attempting to describe them from without, but chooses instead to drift and sketch, in a way that brings out the weight without weighing the text down. Though Fredric Jameson argues that any critical commentary on postmodernism and postmodern culture is 'somehow secretly disarmed and reabsorbed ... since it can achieve no distance from it', Tillman's free-floating fictional inquiry seems able to skate amongst these structures.[42] The conditions might have become too elaborate and all-encompassing to be understood in theoretical terms, but they can still be explored through fiction. Though it might seem more obvious to analyse late capitalism through reference to specific interpretations of commodification, economic theory and social history, fiction does provide a useful way of knowing and interrogating these conditions. Unlike historical or economic texts, fiction can offer speculative and suggestive positions without being required either to prove its hypotheses or substantiate its intuitions. These concerns seem particularly important in the late capitalist period where the attempt to impose a defined theoretical order on the complex and unstable conditions may prove both problematic and intellectually risky. Fiction, and particularly the kind of fiction produced by a writer like Tillman, does something different. Sketching and tracing an image of the world in terms that remain sensitive to its complexities, it manages to communicate a sense of the range of contradictory forces operating in that world.

In these terms the focus on the material dimensions in Tillman's writing can be seen to provide a particularly revealing way of knowing those conditions. Her loose style seems an appropriate vehicle for the representation of a world in which the fluid influence of commodification and economics mixes freely with individual imagination and subjectivity. As Tillman herself argues, fiction creates a space in which 'you don't have to argue as if there's one truth ... you can allow for a lot of ambivalence'.[43] In this fictional domain the text is freed from the constraints imposed by the need to find clear conclusions. This freedom gives her exploration of the contemporary scene a potent interrogative character and enables her to shape her writing in a manner that resists closure and defined positions.

In 'On the Road with Madame Realism', a story from *The Madame Realism Complex* (1992), Tillman describes Andy Warhol's painting of dollar signs and asks, 'is Warhol telling us that money is not "no object"'.[44] Embedded in these remarks is an awareness of the significance of the relationships between the apparently superficial image of the dollar sign and the 'object' it represents. This sensitivity is typical of Tillman's writing and in many ways provides an emblem for her work. The illusion of weightlessness and the sense that there is 'no object' is characteristic of texts which offer a continuous stream of images that trace the links between existence and economics, the aesthetic and the commodity. Her sense of the ways in which human experiences revolve around consumerism provides a link between the arguments developed in this discussion and the ideas raised in the subsequent section, a chapter that looks more precisely at the ways in which blank fiction deals with commodification, and in particular at the brand names, the labels and the commercialised forms of mass culture.

5

Labels

A broad range of mass cultural references is, as the discussion of Lynne Tillman's work has suggested, one of blank fiction's most recognisable characteristics. It must be acknowledged, however, that this kind of writing is not the only contemporary cultural form to incorporate allusions to popular culture. Cross-cultural reference plays a central role in many different kinds of modern American narrative. In contemporary cinema, for example, films like Ethan Cohen's *Barton Fink* (1991), Robert Altman's *The Player* (1992) and Quentin Tarantino's *Pulp Fiction* (1994) all draw heavily on a range of cinematic allusions in narratives that are strewn with interdiscursive references. Tarantino takes cross-cultural allusion to extremes in films that seem heavily dependent on their self-reflexive twists and turns. He adds to this impression by incorporating a whole range of mass cultural references into both *Reservoir Dogs* (1992) and *Pulp Fiction*.[1] Vincent Vega's observations on European hamburgers in *Pulp Fiction* and Mr Pink's analysis of Madonna's 'Like a Virgin' in *Reservoir Dogs* add to the general sense of the relationships between his narratives and their wider cultural context.

Modern cinema's preoccupation with cross-cultural reference is mirrored in contemporary American fiction. Many postwar novelists, including Thomas Pynchon, E.L. Doctorow and Robert Coover, depend on intertextual elements to the extent that these 'metafictional' qualities have come to define much of their work.[2] This interdiscursive impulse is, however, particularly strong in blank fiction, a kind of writing that appears acutely conscious of its position in the contemporary cultural matrix. The work of, for example, Lynne Tillman and Bret Easton Ellis is, like Tarantino's movies, littered with allusions to music, style, advertising, food, fashion and film. Ellis's transtextual focus on the lives of the Bateman brothers in *The Rules of Attraction*, *American Psycho* and, to a lesser extent, *The Informers* (1994) adds weight to this comparison by prompting associations with Tarantino's portrayal of the Vega family in *Reservoir Dogs* and *Pulp Fiction*. Blank fiction is clearly concerned with the implications raised by referentiality and in this concern it articulates a wider preoccupation with the status and significance of mass culture. These allusions form a central part of these texts and need to be interpreted in terms that consider the ways in which they connect this type of writing to its late twentieth-century context.

Intertextuality is often read as a sign of, in Roland Barthes's terms, 'the impossibility of living outside the infinite text', a device that foregrounds the discursive foundations upon which meaning depends.[3] For Linda Hutcheon this interdiscursive strategy prompts 'not only a recognition of textualized traces of the literary and historical past, but also an awareness of what has been done – through irony – to those traces'.[4] Her sense of intertextuality's ironic potential draws heavily on the work of both Barthes and Julia Kristeva and emphasises the critical force generated by what Kristeva describes as discourse's 'multi-stylism and multi-tonality.'[5] This affirmative reading of these processes is countered by critics who share Jameson's sense that cross-cultural pastiche is based on a 'random cannibalisation' of styles and identified as a symptom of cultural de-differentiation.[6] From this point of view, the scatterings of mass cultural allusions in recent fiction serve no purpose, functioning only as the sign of an empty, impotent, postmodern culture. There is no meaning to this range of reference, it is simply incorporated for its own sake. The contrast between these two positions generates reverberations that can be traced in blank fiction's interdiscursive trajectories and can be considered more precisely by looking in detail at Ellis's *Less Than Zero*.

Less Than Zero, Ellis's seminal blank novel, paints a pessimistic portrait of American life in the 1980s, constructing a vision of a seemingly corrupt and meaningless society. The novel describes Christmas in Los Angeles through the eyes of Clay, a listless college student whose life appears to be completed mediated by mass culture and consumption. The narrative describes Clay returning home to California for Christmas from his East Coast university and dropping back into a round of drug-taking and partying with his former school friends. In one scene Clay finds himself in a sushi bar. Ellis writes:

> 'Yeah I like Rockabilly too,' Kim says, wiping her hands. 'But I'm still into the Psychedelic Furs and I like that new Human League song.'
>
> Benjamin says, 'The Human League are out. Over. Finished. You don't know what's going on, Kim.'
>
> Kim shrugs. I wonder where Dimitri is; if Jeff is still holed up with some surfer out in Malibu.
>
> 'No, I mean you really don't,' he goes on. 'I bet you don't even read *The Face*. You've got to.' He lights a clove cigarette. 'You've got to.'
>
> 'Why do you have to?' I ask.
>
> Benjamin looks at me, runs his fingers through his pompadour and says, 'Otherwise you'll get bored.'
>
> I say I guess so.[7]

This section creates the impression that, in Elizabeth Young's words, the characters are 'at the mercy of consumer capitalism, stunned by the storm of signs, codes and simulations'.[8] In the same way that F. Scott Fitzgerald marks Gatsby's superficiality by comparing his personality to the experience of 'skimming hastily through a dozen magazines', Ellis sees shallowness in Benjamin's reverence for *The Face*.[9] The feeling is that Benjamin's trivial preoccupations offer wider insights into contemporary American society's increasing concern for the insubstantial and the insignificant. In this environment, Ellis suggests, the fabric of social identity has been eroded by a culture in which conversations focused on 'The Human League' have more to do with British 'new-wave' than communal experience. From this perspective, *Less Than Zero* is read as a text that offers a satirical commentary on the lives of these privileged teenagers and the society that has nurtured them. This satirical project is fuelled by an implicit hostility towards contemporary culture and an anxiety about conditions in the late twentieth century. Clay's immersion in sushi, surfing and music seems to limit his emotional range and stunt his social development: he, like so many of Ellis's characters, is 'too cool to care' and trapped in a world awash with products, labels, styles and commercial images.[10]

Despite this apparent antagonism, there still appears to be a deep affinity between *Less Than Zero* and popular culture. A novel that draws its title from an Elvis Costello lyric and one of its epigraphs from Led Zeppelin's most famous song reveals a dependence on the dynamics of the popular that inevitably blurs and complicates any satirical design. These complications can be traced in the sushi bar episode, a scene in which Benjamin's desire to follow the fashionable flow is seen to give him a level of connection with his environment and a sense of stability that Clay is unable to equal. Knowing 'what's going on', as far as music and fashion are concerned, is crucial to Benjamin because it keeps him orientated within the fluid currents of popular culture. The confidence he draws from being able to make the right style choice contrasts with Clay's reticence and the equivocality of his sceptical 'I guess so'. When compared to Clay's uncertainty, Benjamin's enthusiasm seems messianic, a suggestion that Ellis strengthens when, in a later section, he shows Clay watching a religious broadcast and listening to the speaker tell him 'you feel confused ... you don't know what's going on'.[11] The echo of Benjamin's insistent words establishes an association between the figures that opens up two possible readings, offering, on the one hand, a comment on the popular's quasi-religious authority, while, on the other, developing a feeling that an understanding of mass culture provides, like religion, a sense of place and purpose.

Even the apparent superficiality represented by Benjamin's reverence for *The Face* can be interpreted in more complex terms. As Dick Hebdidge observes, *The Face* aims to provide '*street credibility, nous*, style tips for those operating within the highly competitive *milieux* of fashion, music and design'.[12] It tells its readers 'how to dance in the dark, how to survive, how to stay on top (on the surface) of things.'[13] These remarks, reflecting once again Benjamin's reverence for style, can be balanced against the kind of critical reading of *The Face* offered by Hebdidge, who, in *Hiding in the Light*, describes it as a magazine that is 'hyperconformist: more commercial than the commercial, more banal than the banal'.[14] Its position within the world of fashion means that it is incorporated into a system in which the sign of commerce holds sway. Its relationship with rebelliousness, street culture and non-conformity is compromised by its participation in a fashion-conscious consumerism that transforms its rebellious iconography into commercialised gestures. Similarly, in *Less Than Zero*, Benjamin's pompadour haircut and interest in 'Rockabilly' seems to mimic a James Dean/Elvis subculture. The problem is, however, that these echoes are only fashion statements. Benjamin's desire to latch on to this fashionable image reveals both his yearning for non-conformity and his assimilation: he is as much a dedicated follower of fashion as a rebel without a cause.

Less Than Zero's contradictory relationship with style, popular culture and the consumerism that underpins these formations can also be traced in its response to MTV and its representation of music video. On a simple level the text seems to regard this particular cultural form as confusingly banal and destructively fragmented. In one scene, early in the novel, Clay finds himself feeling particularly disoriented and turns to MTV for some kind of relief:

> I can still hear people are afraid to merge and I try to get over the sentence, blank it out. I turn on MTV and tell myself I could get over it and go to sleep if I had some Valium and then I think about Muriel and feel a little sick as the videos begin to flash by.[15]

In E. Ann Kaplan's terms, the deterritorialising impact of music video 'blurs distinct separateness and boundaries ... flattening out all the distinct types into one continuous present'.[16] Instead of relieving Clay's anxiety, this 'continuous present' seems to make him feel even more nauseous as the 'videos begin to flash by'. The videos don't help him 'blank' out the anxiety he feels but draw him into a world that actually mirrors the one that originally inspired his disquiet. In the preceding scenes the geography of Los Angeles and Blair's sense of the alienating influence of this environment unsettle

Clay. When Blair observes that 'people are afraid to merge on the freeways of Los Angeles' she gestures towards a wider sense of social fragmentation that Clay is unable to forget.[17] When he turns on MTV he discovers that the juxtaposed images he sees on the screen simply reflect the deracinated conditions of the world outside. The postmodern spaces of Los Angeles are connected to MTV's undifferentiated images and thus Clay finds himself staring at a representation of the forces that disturbed him in the first place.[18]

In these terms, MTV is regarded as a negative force that adds to Clay's sense of disorientation. Ellis's apparent hostility towards music video is developed in *The Informers*, a novel that returns to the Los Angeles of *Less Than Zero* and offers a series of loosely connected stories centred around the lives of a familiar cast of rich-kids. In one section Ellis describes the making of a music video and has the director explain to a member of the band that

> '... I'm just helping you shape your image, okay? Which is of a nice friendly guy from Anaheim who is so fucking lost the mind reels, okay? Let's just do it that way. It took someone four months to write this script – that works out to a month a minute, which is pretty impressive if you think about it – and it's your image,' Martin persists. 'Image, image, image, image.'[19]

The emphasis is on 'image, image, image, image'. The superficial dominates to the extent that 'a month a minute' is regarded as 'pretty impressive'. The impression created in these scenes thus underlines the sense that music video relies on abstractions that erode conceptions of reality and nurture alienation and confusion. Ellis's representation of the power of the image and his description of a cultural form that is determined to show its characters as being 'so fucking lost the mind reels', suggests that as far as Ellis is concerned, MTV is a symptom of some kind of wider social malaise. Ellis seems, like many other commentators, to regard MTV as a 'new snake in the cultural garden'.[20] Clay sits in front of the TV screen passively consuming the messages he sees there. In these images MTV is presented as an opiate, a sedating force created by an industry determined to '*hyperdermically inject* propaganda into the unsuspecting social bloodstream'.[21]

The novel's critical view of this mass cultural formation is, however, compromised by what seems to be Ellis's fascination with MTV and his incorporation of elements of the MTV style into the structure of the novel itself. There are times when Ellis not only alludes to music video, but appears to absorb the characteristically disjointed, episodic qualities of this medium into his writing. In one section, for example, he writes:

> Another video flashes on.
> Julian falls asleep.
> I leave.[22]

The terse presentation of this sequence of events mimics the swift flow of images on MTV and creates the impression that this medium not only reflects the wider environment and influences the imaginations of those living within it, but also affects the way those experiences are narrated. Though on one level Ellis is critical of MTV, on another he seems to explore its creative and expressive possibilities, merging music video with the general communicative function of the text itself. When David Pan argues that Ellis's 'MTV prose style threatens to become as banal as MTV itself', he suggests that Ellis's reliance on these elements degrades the text.[23] Such a view assumes that because he writes like this it must be *bad*, a value judgement that is as negative about MTV as it is about *Less Than Zero*. Though limited from this point of view, Pan's point is interesting insofar as he recognises the importance of the MTV style in Ellis's work. Ellis doesn't simply refer to music video, but actually writes in a way that relies on the stylistic processes of video itself.

This sense of the structural incorporation of the features of music video can be extended by considering *Less Than Zero*'s tendency to eschew clear references to fixed times and places in favour of an approach that locates its events in an empty and eternal present. Though the narration adheres loosely to a straightforward chronological sequence, the episodes are not linked together. The bulk of the text is written in the present tense and many sections are begun without reference to the preceding one. Often Ellis uses the present continuous to introduce the events and, with opening phrases like 'I'm sitting in Du-par's in Studio City' or 'I'm lying in Blair's bed', promotes a feeling of aimlessness and passivity.[24] If Kaplan is correct to argue that MTV offers a vision of a world lived in 'continuous present', then Ellis's approach to organising his novel seems to shadow this atemporal structure. A narrative told in a long undifferentiated stream offers an ideal textual image of a world in which urban space is characterised by a disjointed tangle of freeways and MTV dominates youth culture. The point is however, that while this structural incorporation of MTV seems to compromise any critical agenda, it does not foster a counter perspective that simply celebrates mass culture. *Less Than Zero* appears neither to praise nor blame these formations, but instead enters into a series of diverse and, at times, contradictory relationships with them. Polarised positions are thus disallowed by a text that produces what amounts to a complex dialogue with popular cultures, popular mediums and popular styles. This dialogue can be understood by looking more closely at the function of mass cultural allusions in *Less Than Zero* and considering the status of these references in the text.

This concentration on these elements in *Less Than Zero* moves the focus away from an examination of the text's direct response to contemporary cultural forms and towards a reflection on the implications raised by the novel's incorporation of a wide variety of those forms. Though, in some respects, a novel like *Less Than Zero* can seem empty and uncontextualised, a narrative told, like MTV, in an abstract 'continuous present', the presence of this range of cultural markers gives the novel a very concrete context. The language of the text discloses a specific relationship with the time, space and society of mid 1980s West Coast America. Instead of regarding the presence of this range of mass cultural reference points as a measure of the novel's banality and an index of its weightlessness, these allusions can be interpreted as elements that root the text firmly to a precise material situation.

The scattering of labels, the novel's emphasis on commercial media formations and its obsession with style might on the surface function as the outward and visible signs of a text that is wholly commodified and integrated into the commercial structures of late capitalism. Such a perspective would reflect Mandel's vision of late capitalism and would see in Ellis's novel an image of the all-colonising influence of the late capitalist process. What makes Ellis's text interesting, however, is that even while writing a novel that appears in its very structure to articulate a sense of the particular power and authority of these commercial cultures, he manages, simultaneously, to produce a text that finds a living culture in this commodified world. In this world communication is still possible both despite of and because of the ecstatic confusion of commodities and brand names.

In this way, mass culture and consumerism comes to hold a 'double meaning' for Ellis, a position that reflects that developed by the French theorist Pierre Bourdieu.[25] Bourdieu's work takes exception with interpretations that read the commodity in purely economic terms, arguing that it has both a commercial value *and* a social value. The material status of an object must always be considered alongside an understanding of its expressive function. His emphasis on the commodity's 'double meaning' provides a useful way of interpreting *Less Than Zero*'s use of mass cultural references as for Ellis, like Bourdieu, 'consumer goods lead a double life: as both agents of social control and as objects used by ordinary people in constructing their own culture'.[26] In this way mass culture is seen to articulate significances that are simultaneously material and expressive, commercial and aesthetic. The implication is that Ellis's inclusion of this wide range of allusions to contemporary culture does not bind his text to a sphere that is completely commodified. Instead it connects his writing to elements that articulate a conflicting range of significations. Like commercial culture, the mass cultural references in Ellis's text articulate this double meaning. They express the power and reach of commercial culture while at the same time revealing the ways in which the commodity can be used in an expressive and communicative way. The suggestion is that, without either directly mirroring its social context or trying to establish a purifying distance from that realm, Ellis finds a way of linking his fiction to contemporary conditions. By producing a narrative that relies heavily on contemporary mass cultural references, he creates a text that is able to speak about the experience of living in the contemporary world by using the language of that world.

This discussion of *Less Than Zero*'s language can be developed by looking more closely at the ways in which Ellis loads his texts with reference to products, brand names and commodities. One exemplary section describes Clay's family on a shopping trip for Christmas presents in Beverly Hills:

> My mother has spent most of this time probably at Neiman-Marcus, and my sisters have gone to Jerry Magnin and have used my father's charge account to buy him and me something and then to MGA and Camp Beverly Hills and Privilege to buy themselves something. I sit at the bar at La Scala Boutique bored out of my mind, smoking, drinking red wine. Finally my mother drives up in her Mercedes and parks the car in front of La Scala and waits for me.[27]

The commercial names of the Beverly Hills shopping centres dominate this scene. When Clay's family shop, they shop for 'something'. It's not the purchase that is relevant, it's the point of purchase, the origin. The only important thing is that it's bought in a store with a name. Revealingly Ellis neither attempts to describe what the different stores sell, nor tries to represent their interiors. He simply offers the reader an unadorned list of retail outlets. In the absence of adjectives, qualifying phrases and points of reference, a crucial emphasis is placed on commercial names like 'Neiman-Marcus', 'Jerry Magnin' and 'Camp Beverly Hills'. Ellis is not writing in a way that describes commercial experiences, but developing a prose that is dependent on the very language of commerce and consumerism.

Though capitalism and commodification have often formed the subject matter for American fiction, rarely have novelists used the language of commerce so heavily. Even in *The Great Gatsby* (1926), a novel that seems to prefigure Ellis's interest in the relationship between capitalism and superficiality, commodities don't play such a central role. Gatsby is, it's true, known by what he owns, but still Fitzgerald chooses to describe those possessions rather than label them. Gatsby's fateful car is 'a rich cream colour, bright with nickel, swollen here and there in its monstrous length', a description that though loaded with detail and full of a sense of Gatsby's extravagant wealth, still avoids mentioning the brand.[28] In *Less Than Zero*, however, cars are known not through their appearance but through the name of the manufacturer. Clay's mother drives a 'Mercedes', his psychiatrist a '450 SL', Benjamin a 'BMW 320i'.[29] Where Fitzgerald seems coy about brand and product identity, even though his novel is very obviously concerned with capitalism and consumerism, Ellis produces a style that is 'commodity-heavy'. Size, colour, impression and details are all sidelined in a narrative that prefers to use the maker's name to create the desired effects. In this respect Ellis favours a kind of commercial shorthand, relying on his readership's knowledge of contemporary products to create his effects rather than trying to reproduce impressions through descriptive prose. This, once again, locates the novel very precisely within its particular culture and shows the ways in which Ellis employs the language and signs of his own period as parts of his portrait of that world. He connects his text directly with the ordinary flow of social experience and context by employing the commercial language of the everyday in his descriptions of the commercial scene.

On one level, the presence of these elements suggests that Ellis's style has been completely colonised by commercial interests in the same way that Beverly Hills has been overwhelmed by retail outlets. Unable to differentiate his writing from the flow of commercial culture, Ellis has produced a commodified prose that straightforwardly reflects those conditions. It could even be argued that a novel that includes so much product placement actually strengthens contemporary capitalist structures by promoting further consumerism. Ellis's commodity-heavy style is, however, not as passive or limited as it first appears. Like the novel's engagements with MTV, *The Face* and popular styles, its structural incorporation of the language of consumerism does not symbolise a text that has been completely overwhelmed by commercial conditions. On the contrary, the commodified style works to highlight the text's preoccupation with consumer culture and develops a formal dynamic that supports the narrative's wider negotiations with this complex and contradictory sphere. The language Ellis uses to describe Beverly Hills might be weighed down by commercial associations, but that portrait still retains expressive possibilities. He might be deploying the rhetoric of commodification in a prose style that is bulging with the signs and symbols of consumer culture, but he does not simply provide a straightforward mirror-image of this commercial world.

The emphasis on the contradictions generated by *Less Than Zero*'s style is matched by thematic elements in the text which reveal a similarly complex response to contemporary culture. This situation is apparent in the following description of Clay's restlessness, anxiety and insomnia:

> From my bed, later that night, I can hear the windows throughout the house rattling and I get really freaked out and keep thinking that they're going to crack and shatter. It wakes me and I sit up in bed and look over at the Elvis poster ... the word 'Trust' above his worried face. And then I think about the billboard on Sunset ... finally I fall asleep.[30]

Elvis Costello seems to share Clay's anxiety and, while this does not immediately reassure him, the portrait appears to reduce Clay's sense of isolation and gives him someone to 'Trust'. It is important to understand that this poster is identical with one of the cultural forms that originally contributed to Clay's sense of unease. Earlier in the novel, the 'billboard on Sunset', with its unsettling 'Disappear Here' message, provoked a disquiet that only this new slogan can calm.[31] The negative effect of one mass cultural image is countered by another as Clay finds a cure in the cause.

In sections like these Ellis establishes links between the mass cultural matrix and the identity of his character. This position is underlined in Clay's speech which appears studded with catch-phrases that he's gleaned from the flow of culture around him. 'Disappear here', 'afraid to merge', 'I wonder if he's for sale' and 'what's going on?' are slogans that he returns to repeatedly.[32] These clichés dominate his language and create the impression of a mind that is both deeply influenced by external impressions and wholly caught up in communicative codes that have more to do with the repetitive slogans and commercial choruses of advertising than the demands of personal expression. This point is developed in Ellis's later novel *The Rules of Attraction*, a narrative in which Clay's reappearance provides an opportunity for Ellis to mock this use of catch-phrases:

Someone from L.A. sent me a video-tape, unmarked ... I have lost my I.D. three times this term ... I ... started taking an advanced video course ...
    Someone asks me: 'What's going on?'
    'I don't know,' I say. 'What *is* going on?'
    Sensory Deprivation Tank.
    Rest in Peace.
    People are afraid to merge on campus after midnight.[33]

In this section Clay seems increasingly confused and uncertain. The familiar anxiety about the impact of the visual media is crystallised in his response to the unmarked video tape. This sinister object threatens his precarious identity, as does the loss of his 'I.D.' card. After revealing that he is taking an 'advanced video course', Clay's confessions become completely disjointed and collapse into a series of unconnected comments. The suggestion is that Clay's precarious mental condition appears to be connected to his contact with these visual media, a link that underpins Ellis's use of a form that depends on the banalities of a series of interchangeable slogans. Like Sean Bateman's use of the repeated phrases 'Rock 'n' Roll' and 'deal with it' in the same novel, Clay finds himself unable to produce an individualised language and can only rely on these tired, blank constructions.[34] The point is, however, that despite the clichéd nature of the language used by characters like Sean Bateman and Clay, they still manage to communicate and find a way of expressing themselves in what is, in a sense, a mass cultural argot. Like their repeated emphasis on brand names, labels and consumer objects, these phrases provide them with a way of communicating and establishing their identities. On the one hand, a character like Clay appears to have been overwhelmed by the commercial world in which he is living, while on the other, he seems to have appropriated various elements from it and turned them around for his own purposes.

Less Than Zero's relationship with mass culture thus seems based in a sophisticated sense of the popular's conflicting range of significations. In this way Ellis's text shadows the theoretical discussion of popular culture offered by, among others, Tony Bennett. Bennett's argument is that the popular needs to be conceived

> neither as the site of the people's deformation, nor as that of their cultural self-affirmation, or, in any simple Thompsonian sense, of their own self-making; rather, it is viewed as a force field of relations shaped, precisely, by ... contradictory pressures and tendencies.[35]

Unlike perspectives that understand contemporary culture as a closed, rigid and integrated space, Bennett draws on ideas developed in Antonio Gramsci's *Selections from Prison Notebooks* to produce an approach that sees the popular as a site in which a number of competing forces intersect. Bennett's analysis of culture's dependency both on the logic of the producer and on the concerns of the consumer has clear echoes of Bourdieu. Like Bourdieu, Bennett recognises the ways in which commercial culture bears the traces of the clash between the dominant and the subordinate. The commodity is marked by a conflict between commercial interests and consumer priorities, a tension that gives these cultural forms a variety of competing significances. This situation is dramatised in *Less Than Zero*, a novel that, while offering a vision of a world dominated by an increasingly commodified culture, finds itself still able to recognise the cracks and contradictions in this supposedly totalised edifice. Bennett's argument thus provides a way of reading *Less Than Zero* that parallels the positions developed in the discussion of Ellis's commercial language. The novel seems to be engaged in a series of negotiations with the popular and through these processes develops a dialogue with the cultural and material conditions in late twentieth-century America.

From this perspective, the use of cross-cultural reference in Ellis's text can be interpreted in a manner that departs from familiar readings of interdiscursivity as a classically postmodern kind of pastiche. This departure is complicated, however, by elements in the text that seem to encourage interpretations developed within the terms of the postmodernism debate. On one level the characters described in *Less Than Zero* seem to be straightforward representations of the postmodern jet-set described by Jean-Francois Lyotard, an impression strengthened by the text's repeated emphasis on postmodern cultural forms like the geography of Los Angeles, fast food and MTV.[36] These features have fostered approaches that read the text as a simple literalisation of Baudrillard's hyperreal, or regard it as an image of a postmodern world that seems, from a Jamesonian perspective, all-embracing. *Less Than Zero*, in terms that return to positions outlined in earlier parts of this discussion, is thus identified as a text that simultaneously reflects postmodern conditions while replicating and reproducing those conditions. The text's descriptions of characters lost in a fluid postmodern culture, an environment in which their reference points appear to have been destroyed, supports this kind of approach and fosters comparisons that link Ellis's vision to the theoretical positions offered by these postmodern theorists.

Compelling though this perspective may be, there is a sense in which the mass cultural references in Ellis's text can be seen to articulate a more complex view of contemporary conditions, one that undermines these 'overly totalizing' visions.[37] Instead of regarding American culture as a static structure that simply expresses conditions in late capitalism, *Less Than Zero* rejects this monolithic conception by portraying experiences that are 'too complex and confusing' to permit 'the simple labelling of cultural products as "progressive" or "reactionary"'.[38] While Ellis's novel shares Jameson's understanding of the increasingly commodified character of contemporary culture and echoes Baudrillard's thoughts on the heightened significance of simulation, it does not match their belief that these are the dominant, defining and incontestable features of contemporary experience. As the incorporation of this range of mass cultural references shows, there is still room for manoeuvre: consumers of popular culture aren't necessarily the passive victims of late capitalism's cultural logic.

These positions are brought to the fore in *Less Than Zero*'s final pages, a section in which Clay finds himself drawn towards an increasingly apocalyptic vision. In an echo of Nathanael West's conclusion to *The Day of the Locust* (1939), Ellis imagines the destruction of Los Angeles. The difference is, however, that where West sees this fire as a purifying event, Ellis's writing is unable to differentiate this apocalypse from the forces which precipitated the crisis in the first place. Once again, like the rest of his experiences, Clay's perceptions are totally mediated through mass culture:

> There was a song I heard when I was in Los Angeles by a local group. The song was called 'Los Angeles' and the words and images were so harsh and bitter that the song would reverberate in my mind for days ... Images of people, teenagers my own age, looking up from the asphalt and being blinded by the sun. Images so violent and malicious that they seemed to be my only point of reference for a long time afterwards. After I left.[39]

These mass cultural allusions provide Clay's 'only point of reference' and it is around them that he constructs his experience. In this concluding section it is popular culture that gives Clay a way of understanding his situation. The image, figured as a degrading force in other parts of the text, is thus regarded, in this final movement, in a much less critical light. When, at the end of his vacation, Clay clears out his room, he observes that

> There was nothing much left ... except a couple of books, the television, stereo, the mattress, the Elvis Costello poster ... There was also a poster of California ... one of the pins had fallen out and the poster was old and torn down the middle and was tilted and hanging unevenly from the wall.[40]

The sense of doom conveyed here appears, in one way, to be linked to the decadent and destructive world depicted in the text. The novel has described a corrupt and image-obsessed society 'torn down the middle'. The point is, however, that in order to express this despair, Ellis finds himself drawn towards using the very forces that he has identified as having been partially responsible for the catastrophe. In many ways the poster stands as an image for the whole novel which, despite using commercialised forms and images, still manages to produce a portrait of a society that is 'hanging unevenly from the wall'. Like the eyes of T.J. Eckleberg in *The Great Gatsby*, Elvis Costello looks down on this ruined world, a world which he, in part, has helped to create.[41] Fitzgerald's image of a commercial god (Eckleberg) gazing down over the ruined wastes of early twentieth-century commercialism is thus replayed in *Less Than Zero*, a novel that shares Fitzgerald's sense of the circuits that connect the literary imagination to the wider currents of mass culture and capitalism.

This sense of the implications raised by *Less Than Zero*'s incorporation of a wide spread of mass cultural allusions can be developed by considering the ways in which other blank fictions include popular reference and, in particular, references to punk. Like music video, brand names and styles, punk is a culture which seems to have a clear significance and its presence in contemporary fiction would appear to align those texts with a defined anti-establishment ethos. The punk elements in this kind of narrative look, on the surface, like the marks of what could be described as a punk fiction. Indeed Young and Caveney have emphasised blank fiction's 'necessary link with punk'.[42] This link, however, is potentially misleading as the presence of punk in these novels does not necessarily mean that they share punk's adversarial spirit. The characters in *Less Than Zero* might pull on punk clothes and listen to the music, but there is no sense in which they might be called punks.

A similar situation is described in Dennis Cooper's *Closer* (1992), a text which, like the rest of Cooper's fiction, is set in the Californian sprawl and focused on the experiences of a group of gay adolescents. Punk's importance in the narrative emerges in Cooper's portrait of John, a young artist who has created an identity for himself out of punk:

> Six years ago punk had focused his life ... he dyed his hair blue-black, wore torn T-shirts, smeared his eyes with mascara

and stared at the floors of his school ... He'd never felt more comfortable in his life.[43]

This section raises immediate questions about the status of punk in the text by associating this supposedly antagonistic subculture with being 'comfortable'. The oxymoronic idea of the comfortable punk generates tensions between the established image of punk as a stylistic risk and this more mundane sense of it as a source of security and identity.

The uncertainty surrounding punk's status finds a more brutal expression when John meets another punk and enters into a violent sexual relationship with him. While abusing the punk, John observes that this 'bleeding punk kid ... [is] horrific and ridiculous and sort of moving too'.[44] In this scene John appears to be attacking his own self-image and undermining the identity from which he has drawn so much apparent comfort. The text thus represents his punk identity in terms that lack the clear, adversarial thrust normally associated with this particular subculture. There is obviously a link with punk, but that link gives the text neither a critical edge nor a uniform cultural significance. On the contrary, punk's status in *Closer* seems unstable, lacking what Dick Hebdidge has described as punk's 'grim determination ... to detach itself from normalised forms'.[45] Instead of an anti-establishment position, *Closer's* representation of punk produces a more complex vision in which its critical direction is balanced against an understanding of its more conservative elements. As Sadie Plant suggests, punk

came to operate as a social safety-valve: once people got used to ripped jeans, safety pins and mohican haircuts, the public became almost thankful that the rebellion was not more intrusive. Indeed, punk was accommodated so quickly that the possibility was raised that it was incorporated before it had even begun.[46]

Closer brings forward a sense of punk's ambiguity and presents it as a style that is simultaneously radical and recuperated. In Plant's terms, punk is not a uniformly critical subculture, but one in which antagonistic accents clash with affirmative ones. Cooper's vaguely punkish rich-kids are emblematic of these contradictions and represent the ambiguous identities the characters draw from the popular cultural matrix. *Closer* is not a punk novel but a novel with punk in it. Its cross-cultural references produce a range of diverging significations and, as a result, offer an insight into both the complexity of mass cultural forms and, by implication, a sense of the contradictions that characterise contemporary culture as a whole.

Closer's representation of punk is fairly typical of blank fiction's negotiations with popular culture and contemporary style and the similarities between Cooper's positions and those offered in *Less Than Zero* are easy to find. Clay may wear ripped jeans and listen to new-wave punk bands like X and Devo, but he is not a punk and always finds himself, like John, unable to identify completely. These problematic relationships can be placed in a more general context by considering the ill-suitedness of the punk ethos to the culture of privileged, '80s American youth described by both Cooper and Ellis. Punk's sentiments are both anti-materialist and anti-American and it was no coincidence that the spirit of punk, distilled among disaffected youths in London, was evaporated by America's glare, conditions that left Sid Vicious dead in New York and Johnny Rotten rich and aimless in Los Angeles. It is also important to recognise that punk is a phenomenon that predates the emergence of blank fiction by at least five years. Punk's moment was between 1976 and 1978, while blank fiction emerged in the mid 1980s and developed too late to have any direct relationship with punk.

It is possible to extend these ideas by considering the similarities between the representation of punk in *Less Than Zero* and *Closer* and the way punk and post-punk styles are incorporated into 'Betrayed by David Bowie', a story from Lev Raphael's *Dancing on Tisha B'Av* (1990) collection. The stories in *Dancing on Tisha B'Av* are typically campus-based tales about Jewish men coming out and dealing with the tensions generated by the clash between gay desire and Jewish moral codes and traditions. 'Betrayed by David Bowie' offers a variation on these themes by using the polymorphous and androgynous nature of David Bowie's public persona as a register for the fluctuating emotional states experienced by two gay students involved in a formative affair. For the narrator,

Whether Bowie was bi or gay, what made him the greatest for me was that he said he liked men, and did it openly, in the press. It permeated his songs. He was exotic, he was brilliant, he was strong, and Jeff and I wanted to be as cool as the sax on the *Pin-Ups* covers, as lewd as the boys who 'suck you while you're sleeping', as funky and dreamy as 'Fascination'.[47]

The affair collapses when Jeff's reluctance to confront his own sexuality creates unresolvable tensions in the relationship. Jeff's attitude is shadowed by a reflection on Bowie's sexual transformations in the early 1980s. The narrator considers the media coverage of the 'David Bowie Straight' revelations and describes how 'suddenly everybody, including Bowie, was saying that the androgyny, the bisexuality, had only been poses'.[48] What the narrator regards as David Bowie's betrayal is thus aligned with Jeff's uneasy response to his own sexual desires. The narrator offers a commentary on betrayal and authenticity. He assumes that Bowie had a 'real' sexual identity and uses the discovery of Bowie's 'inauthenticity' as a way of assessing his former partner's attitude. On a more complex level, however, he misses the point of Bowie's complex post-punk posturing and fails to grasp Bowie's contempt for the whole concept of the authentic, or appreciate his acts of self-reinvention. The narrator's yearning for an uncontradictory Bowie leads him into these difficulties and emphasises the problem with trying to establish stable coordinates within popular culture.

It is important to recognise, however, that Bowie's rejection of authenticity does not make his gestures either empty or meaningless. Cultural figures like him may lack the kind of stable values the narrator desires, but instead they find identity in fluidity. As Richard Dyer argues in his work on movie icons, stars are engaged in the process of not only 'shoring up the notion of the individual but also, at times, registering doubts and anxieties attendant upon it'.[49] What is interesting about the use of Bowie in this story is that while the narrator is lamenting his lack of consistency, the piece itself incorporates the variety of possible significances generated by the star and uses them as a way of articulating the complexities of sexual identity. In these terms, Bowie is appropriated into the structure of the text and used to signal the ambiguity and contingency of social, personal and sexual identities. Raphael's story thus, in its content, seems to mourn the passing of stability, while in its form appears to depend on the mutability of Bowie as a cultural signifier. This has a particular importance for this discussion, because, as Richard Dyer suggests, stars are 'involved in making themselves into commodities; they are both the labour and the thing the labour produces'.[50] The point is, however, that this commercial aspect neither means these signs hold a wholly negative range of significances nor suggests that their presence in a text of this kind marks that text as the product of a thoroughly mercantile culture. On the contrary, the commodity, in this case David Bowie, is drawn into the language of the text and its meanings located within a scheme that produces an image of complex kinds of cultural experience.

Though this argument has offered a plural reading of the range of mass cultural allusions offered in blank fiction, concerns remain about the ways in which the inclusion of commercial languages and imagery drawn from advertising might provide a much more straightforward portrait of a text that is directly integrated into the commercial structures of late capitalist society. This impression is nurtured by the perception that advertising messages are imbued with a manipulative power and the feeling that these images are, unlike other cultural forms, strongly focused around a linear logic dictated by the demands of product promotion. Critics as diverse as W.F. Haug, Vance Packard and Sut Jhally have all reflected on advertising's power and its capacity to shape and mould the consumer's habits, dreams and aspirations. In these terms, the incorporation of the language and imagery of marketing into blank fiction would appear to be a sign of both advertising's ability to influence and control and late capitalism's colonising power. The problem with this position is that it fails to take into account the ways in which the advertiser's message is always consumed in a manner that actually brings a variety of competing values into play. In Judith Williamson's terms, advertising relies on 'structures of meaning' and requires symbolic interpretations based on a variety of different codes and associations that leads to the inevitable disruption of the unity of the intended message.[51] Although the inclusion of advertising icons in blank fictions creates the impression that these are texts dominated by commercial forces, this analysis of the contradictory nature of the advertising image provides a way of thinking about these incorporations in terms of disruption.

This situation is dramatised in Ellis's *The Rules of Attraction*. Paul Denton, Sean Bateman's spurned lover, describes how when 'watching TV nothing makes sense. An Acutrim commercial is followed by a Snickers commercial followed by a Kinks video followed by In the News.'[52] In this section he registers his awareness of the disjunctions and fragmentations that characterise the medium. His perspective is balanced against a feeling that he is, despite his blank response, being reached by the corporate messages he is observing. Perhaps they are not reaching him in the way that they were originally intended to, but they are still influencing his consciousness and entering his imagination. He can remember the brand names and he can differentiate each visual sequence despite the fact that nothing 'makes sense'. It is this clash between his immersion in the flow of commercial images and his grasp of the absurdity of the spectacle that creates the disjunction and marks the distance between him and the ideal of the integrated, acquiescent consumer. Denton's separation thus becomes a model for the text itself, symbolising the distance Ellis establishes between the commercialism of the world he describes and the terrains of his own fiction. He is caught up in this capitalist maelstrom, but still manages to find a way of representing it without becoming totally absorbed in its commercial processes.

This method is taken to an even more extreme level by Mark Leyner, who, in the novels *My Cousin My Gastroenterologist* (1990) and *Et Tu, Babe* (1993), explores the extremities of Californian commercial culture to produce extravagant comic narratives that ridicule and destabilise the overblown commercial structures of late capitalism. His vision is one that mixes commodification with anarchic, liberating elements to produce a kind of free-floating prose that exceeds all regulation. In one typically exuberant section from *Et Tu, Babe*, the novel's narrator find himself on a plane

> seated next to a fascinating passenger. She's Flo, a chimpanzee selected by Jane Goodall from among chimps at Tanzania's Gombe National Park, who was taught a sign language vocabulary of over 2,000 words. Flo often appears on MacNeil-Leher, 'Nightline' with Ted Koppel, and CNN, participating in panel discussions on animal rights ... Luckily I learned sign language when I dated the Academy Award-winning deaf actress Marlee Matlin when I lived in L.A., so communicating with Flo is no problem. I learn that she's flying to the states to 'speak' at a demonstration against a new product that's been introduced by Burger Hut called Rhesus Pieces: bite size chunks of rhesus monkey coated in granola and deep-fried.[53]

In this stream of references to products, personalities and marketing opportunities Leyner manages to develop a perspective that sees a curious life in the signs and symbols of late twentieth century commercial culture. Phrases like 'Academy Award-winning' and 'bite-size chunks' link his text with the hackneyed tones of the tabloid, a style that connects the novel to the currents of commercial culture. Leyner's prose, however, has a hyperbolic intensity that frees it from these constraints. His text finds a paradoxical position that is both immersed in and separate from the flow of commercial culture. Like Leyner, Ellis also manages to find this kind of unstable position. For both novelists, the profusion of mass cultural imagery and commercial references function neither as symptoms of the unquestionable domination of the commodity nor as the marks of an aesthetic style that is tied to the priorities of consumer society, but as features that enable their narratives to explore the significances generated by these mass cultural formations.

Like the free-floating consumerism of Tillman's narrator in *Motion Sickness*, the incorporation of mass cultural allusions in the work of Ellis, Leyner, Cooper and Raphael are seen as elements that, far from identifying their texts with the controlling structures of late capitalism, actually produce a sense of the indeterminacy and fluidity of experiences in contemporary culture. Where Tillman's narrator found the freedom to consume without finding her identity colonised by commodification, these narratives show the ways in which it is possible to engage with mass culture without being integrated and incorporated by these supposedly rigid and commercial experiences. The exuberance of Mark Leyner's writing and the destructive visions of Clay are particularly interesting as they provide a way of linking the ideas developed in this chapter with the analysis of the significance of millennial anxieties in blank fiction that occupies the final pages of this discussion. The brand-heavy styles and overloaded commercial prose of these writers generate an apocalyptic atmosphere that provides a way of conceiving the relationship between these patterns and blank fiction's representations of decadence.

6

Decadence

The gloomy tones that colour Clay's bitter portrait of Los
Angeles at the end of *Less Than Zero* are typical of the kind of
apocalyptic elements that pattern blank fiction. These
destructive themes have provided a continual point of
reference for this discussion and cast a disturbing shadow
over blank fiction. In most of these narratives there is no
relief, no real revelation or redemption, only a profoundly
depressing sense of impending destruction. The fictional
worlds these texts represent seem clouded by millennial
anxieties and touched by the violent, destructive and decadent
currents of what has been described as the 'apocalypse culture'
of the late twentieth century.[1] Blank fiction's emphasis on what
appears to be a culture plagued by *fin de siècle* concerns
demands interpretation, an analysis that can be contextualised
by exploring the significance of this 'apocalypse culture'.

Contemporary culture seems increasingly preoccupied with the
millennium. 'Endism', the cult of the end, casts a familiar
shadow.[2] The cooling of the Cold War may have calmed fears
about impending nuclear apocalypse, but the threat of
environmental Armageddon and the activities of millenarian
sects provide new sources of anxiety. Academic texts, including
Robert Sinai's *The Decadence of the Modern World* (1978), Joe
Bailey's *Pessimism* (1988), Richard Dellamora's *Apocalyptic
Overtures* (1994) and Francis Fukuyama's *The End of History*
(1989), echo this apocalyptic atmosphere. One of the most
striking versions of the endist thesis is offered by Alain Minc
who, in *Le Nouveau Moyen Âge* (1993), suggests that modernity's
dream of a clean, well-lighted place is being supplanted by a
return to the fear and superstition that characterised the middle
ages. This entropic vision is sustained by a series of obvious
comparisons between the anxieties of the contemporary period

and those of the *fin de siècle*. Elaine Showalter's *Sexual Anarchy* details some of the points of comparison and produces an argument that sees a strong image of the past in her vision of the present.[3] Showalter makes a great deal of, for example, the similarity between the nineteenth-century furore generated by syphilis and the contemporary moral panic surrounding HIV and AIDS.[4] Showalter's argument establishes further parallels between the two epochs by identifying connections between the urban conditions in late Victorian Britain and the experiences of the poor in modern metropoli.[5] Homelessness, she suggests, was as much a feature of *fin de siècle* London as it is of late twentieth-century New York. These links provide the foundations for Showalter's argument, a perspective that Stjepan Mestrovic reflects on in *The Coming Fin de Siècle* when he suggests that the 'conditions at the end of this century are not essentially different from those of the previous one'.[6]

Comparisons between AIDS and syphilis are, however, more attractive than they are productive and, likewise, the desire to interpret modern urban problems through the prism of the past seems to beg as many questions as it answers. Showalter's thesis is marked by what Gillian Beer calls 'presentism', an approach that reads the past in terms of the present and, as a result, finds itself unable to offer specific insights into either epoch.[7] These criticisms must be tempered by an appreciation of the attractive nature of arguments based on the comparison between the two periods. Showalter's position is seductive and its appeal is strengthened by the presence of further similarities between the *fin de siècle* anxieties of the nineteenth century and those of the contemporary period. Reflections on the degrading impact of mass culture and, in particular, the mass media are as common in the late twentieth century as they were a hundred years ago. Matthew Arnold's defence of the high cultural citadel against a marauding horde of barbarians has contemporary resonances that anybody who has seen Oliver Stone's *Natural Born Killers* will recognise.[8] It is, however, difficult to anchor these kinds of critiques either to the beginning or the end of the twentieth century and, as a result, questions must be asked about readings that attempt to interpret these critiques as precise expressions of *fin de siècle* fears. As Aldous Huxley's *Brave New World* (1932), George

Orwell's *Nineteen Eighty-Four* (1949), Ray Bradbury's *Fahrenheit 451* (1953) and David Cronenberg's *Videodrome* (1982) illustrate, gloomy meditations on the influence of popular culture pattern the last hundred years with a regularity that undermines arguments aimed at isolating an apocalyptic hundred-year-itch. It was Veblen in 1919 who identified the enduring quality of cultural jeremiads and recognised the contemporary significance of Juvenal's complaint about the degraded and apolitical character of Imperial Rome.[9] Rome, Juvenal argued, was a place where the mass's only concern was for the sensory pleasures of 'bread and the circuses'.[10] Veblen saw the relevance of Juvenal's words to his own time and linked the ancient's desire for bread and circuses with the 'breadlines' and 'movies' of his own period.[11]

The point is that intimations of impending apocalypse haunt almost every decade of every century in a way that problematises the attempt to identify these fears as specific manifestations of millennial concern. From this perspective, the idea of the decaying society and the significance of the *fin de siècle* is seen to depend more on perceived realities than historical facts. The lure of millennial thinking is potent enough to create this enormous range of discourses, but efforts to link these discourses to material conditions are inevitably problematic.[12] Every age, it seems, bears witness to its own decline and, as a result, the idea of the millennium needs to be treated sceptically, especially when looking for ways of explaining particular cultural phenomena.

These criticisms of millennial mythologies provide the background for a discussion of the role played by *fin de siècle* concerns in blank fiction. The apocalyptic mood generated in many of these texts can be linked to what appears to be the fundamentally decadent atmosphere produced by fiction of this kind. The general sense of wastefulness and *ennui* developed in blank fiction fuels this apprehension, a perception that is strengthened by texts that seem to be weighed down with *fin de siècle* themes and associations. The figure of the vampire, that staple of nineteenth-century decadent fictions, can be found once more in contemporary texts like Ellis's recent *The Informers* and also in the more obscure work of Kathe Koja and Poppy Z. Brite. In blank fiction's revivification of the vampire myth lies the suggestion that it, like *fin de siècle* writing, has a specific interest in themes related to plague, disease and contamination, a suggestion that finds more conscious evocation in narratives that touch specifically on AIDS, like David Wojnarowicz's *Close to the Knives* (1992), Jay McInerney's *Brightness Falls* and Susan Sontag's blank novella *The Way We Live Now* (1986).

This sense of the specific thematic similarities between blank fiction and the decadent writing of the nineteenth century can be strengthened by considering the ways in which its interests in experimentation with sex, narcotics and gender parallel the concerns of nineteenth-century *fin de siècle* narrative. There appears to be something very obviously decadent in the blank descriptions of sexual extremism and over-indulgence offered in the fiction of, for example, Dennis Cooper, a writer whose novels appear motivated by what Roger Clarke identifies as the author's desire to see 'spiritual decay ... lovingly dissected.'[13] In similar terms an early review of McInerney and Ellis identified them as 'two divine decadents', a perspective that is echoed in Matthew Tyrnauer's sense of the ways in which Ellis's novels offer visions of a culture in which the 'sense of anomie is heightened ... the clock seems to be winding down'.[14] The impression created by these remarks is that there are strong links between blank fiction and decadence. These connections raise a number of important issues, with the most significant being a concern about both the validity and the usefulness of comparisons between the *fin de siècle* of nineteenth-century Europe and the character of contemporary American narrative. The central questions are: is blank fiction decadent (with all the *fin de siècle* associations that this decadence would bring with it) and, if so, what does the presence of these decadent themes signify?

While the identification of thematic links between blank fiction and decadent writing gestures towards the presence of a connection between the two, these similarities offer no conclusive proof. The presence of the vampire in blank fiction does not necessarily mean that this is a decadent type of writing, it simply means that it is a type of writing that is aware of decadent iconography. More significantly, the deployment of these thematic connections makes it very easy to look back on *fin de siècle* fiction and offer a lazy reading of contemporary narratives as simple re-enactments of the strategies of the past. The obvious danger with such an approach is that interpretation of the specific characteristics of each literary project will be replaced by a bland and unproductive sense of similitude.

The problems with simple comparisons of this kind can be avoided by producing a more sophisticated interpretation of nineteenth-century decadent fiction and developing a detailed understanding of what the term decadence actually means. The typical characteristics of *fin de siècle* writing can be traced in the introspective and self-indulgent tone of texts like *Against Nature* (1884) and *The Picture of Dorian Gray* (1890). In these narratives a great emphasis is placed on the process of withdrawing from society and the importance of living life at one remove from nature and reality.[15] The protagonists seek out rarefied experiences and try to satisfy Walter Pater's demand that life be lived 'passionately', fuelled by epicurean tastes for 'strange dyes, strange colours, [and] curious odours'.[16] The decadent quest for unusual pleasures is shadowed by the narrative's formal concern for 'jewelled ornamentation' and 'the rare word'.[17] This fetishisation of elaborate language can be linked to Gayatri Spivak's wider sense of the decadent style as 'a way of writing where the references seem to be not to a world of nature but always to a world already made into artifice.'[18] It is this preoccupation with the artificial that defines the decadent project, an enterprise that finds a place for what Baudelaire calls the 'love of deceit'.[19]

The fundamentally introspective character of *fin de siècle* writing reveals a general hostility towards the material world. This hostility can be interpreted by reflecting on the social and economic uncertainties that characterised late nineteenth-century life. This was a period marked by change: gender roles, the colonial structure and the capitalist mode of production were all undergoing significant transformations.[20] These shifts generated a feeling of insecurity which fuelled millennial speculation and heightened concerns about degeneration. In response to these apparently unstable and threatening conditions, European writers sought refuge in art and tried to use the decadent aesthetic as a barrier between themselves and an increasingly confusing external world.[21]

Despite the problems with this thumbnail sketch of literary decadence, it introduces a general sense of the role played by material conditions in the development of *fin de siècle* narrative and offers a particular insight into decadent writing's relationship with changes in the economic structure. The shift from market to monopoly capitalism in the later half of the nineteenth century heightened concerns about the alienating impact of this kind of economic structure and added urgency to the search for uncommodified experiences.[22] This pursuit is explored in greater detail in *Charles Baudelaire: A Lyric Poet in the Era of High-Capitalism* where Walter Benjamin argues that Baudelaire's use of the lyric mode constitutes a return to a precapitalist form that has the capacity to resist the mercantile encroachments of high capitalism. In Benjamin's terms, Baudelaire's work turns Paris into the 'subject of lyrical poetry' and thus, using this form, finds a way of bestowing 'a conciliatory gleam over the growing destitution of men in the great city'.[23] Despite this optimistic tone there are, however, contradictions in this 'conciliatory' project, contradictions that develop because, as Benjamin makes clear, the act of appropriating lyric poetry and mobilising it against the commodifying impact of high capitalism is itself a gesture that mimics the very mechanisms of appropriation that are central to the process of commodification.[24] This paradox creates a situation in which the lyrical figure of the *flâneur* can only escape alienation by creating an illusion and, in Benjamin's terms, 'filling the hollow space created in him by ... isolation with the borrowed ... isolations of strangers'.[25] In this reading these processes seem to work against their original intention, bringing not relief from the mercantile world but actually a more profound engagement with it: 'the intoxication to which the *flâneur* surrenders is the intoxication of the commodity'.[26]

This kind of paradox typifies the decadent project. The refined tastes of figures like Dorian Gray and Des Esseintes are, like Baudelaire's lyric poetry, intended to signify the rejection of the base world of commerce. The difficulty is that these desires are, at the same time, manifestations of a consumerist yearning for sensory indulgence. When reading *Against Nature*, for example, it is hard to escape the fact that the protagonist is a privileged individual whose withdrawal from the real world and quest for refined aestheticised experiences are intimately linked to profound yearnings for luxurious and perfectly packaged products. As Rosalind Williams argues, 'despite ... [Des Esseintes's] desperate attempts to exclude the values of the marketplace from Fonterey, they remain potent, acting like invisible magnetic poles casting a field of force over his life, relentlessly pulling and distorting all his feelings and choices'.[27] In *Against Nature*, Williams suggests, Des Esseintes's escapist urges are ironically transformed into an expression of the power from which he is attempting to escape. The harder he tries to free himself from the constraints of commodified culture, the more he finds himself trapped within them. It is important to recognise, however, that the decadent project isn't completely undermined by this central contradiction. On the contrary, an appreciation of the futility of the enterprise can, in a curious way, be regarded as a source of its strength.[28] The inevitable failure of the project outlined in a novel like *Against Nature* is, in a sense, fundamental to its success for, in this futility, it manages to reach an even more profoundly decadent pitch.

This review of nineteenth-century decadence's relationship with commodification provides a framework within which a more specific reading of the possible links between this literary mode and late twentieth-century forms like blank fiction can be produced. Unlike the superficial connections between the thematic foci of *fin de siècle* European writing and the contemporary American novel, this understanding of decadence as a response to changes in the mode of production offers a means of connecting the two forms in a way that actually compares like with like. As this discussion has argued, blank fiction can be interpreted in terms that trace the links between its textual strategies and the dynamics of late capitalism. This position provides the terms around which more substantial comparisons between this type of contemporary American fiction and the writing of nineteenth-century Europe can be built. In the same way that the emergence of nineteenth-century decadence is interpreted as an imaginative dilemma generated by the change from market to monopoly capitalism, blank fiction is read in relation to the change from monopoly capitalism to late capitalism. This approach has two advantages: it neither depends on an argument that compares two literary modes that, coincidentally, emerged at the end of consecutive centuries, nor hinges on a contrast between types of writing that both happen to include references to vampires, disease and sexual experimentation. Instead it produces a reading that links texts that appear to articulate a similar response to shifts in the economic organisation of their respective societies.

A more specific perspective on these relationships can be developed by looking in greater detail at the ways in which decadence is represented in blank fiction. Like *Less Than Zero* and *American Psycho*, Ellis's *Rules of Attraction* includes a number of elements that appear to link the text to a decadent sensibility. The novel describes the tangled relationships that develop between Sean, Paul and Lauren, three rich, idle students. Their three-way affair is set against the background of East Coast American college life and offers a shifting portrait of privilege, indolence, sexual mores and lazy indulgence. In *The Rules of Attraction*, the students sleep with each other, take drugs, drink and spend their substantial allowances without seeming to pay any attention to the academic demands of college life. Like Fonterey for Des Esseintes, the fictional environment of Camden College provides a sequestered space for their decadent explorations. In one characteristic scene Paul meets up with Richard, an old family friend, and is surprised by his appearance:

> His long blond hair is now short, cropped and dyed a bright platinum blond that, because of the rain or mousse, looks dark. He's wearing a ripped white tuxedo shirt, one black sock, one white sock, and black Converse hi-Tops, and a long overcoat with a Siouxi and the Banshees decal stuck on the back. A tiny diamond stud earring in the left ear, the Wayfarers still on, black and shiny. He's only carrying one small black bag with Dead Kennedys and Bronski Beat

stickers on it, and in the other hand a very large cassette player and a bottle of Jack Daniel's, almost empty.[29]

Links between the commodity strewn descriptions that characterise the rest of Ellis's novels are obvious in this scene. The important point as far as this particular section is concerned is that the stylistic references can be interpreted in terms drawn from analysis of the nineteenth-century posturing of the dandy. Richard, with his extravagant clothes, seems to be trying to use his appearance as a way of signalling his contempt for the mundane currents of everyday life. Echoes of Dorian Gray's and Des Esseintes's epicurean tastes reverberate in Ellis's description of Richard's consumption of British post-punk music, fashion, hair-styles, electronic goods and alcohol. In these terms he seems intent on turning himself into a kind of late twentieth-century dandy.

This position can be linked to the perspectives on punk developed in the preceding chapter and reference made to the way in which both Richard and punks in general seem, in terms borrowed from Hebdidge's analysis, to be trying to 'present themselves as "degenerates", as signs of ... highly publicized decay'.[30] What makes Richard's punk gestures particularly decadent is the way in which he attempts to project this degenerate image using commercial symbols. Where, as Ellen Moers suggests, 'Baudelaire brought out all the capacity of the dandy figure for rebellion: for scornful, silent, unsuccessful rebellion against the mediocre materialism of the democratic era', Richard attempts to shift and mutate the symbols of commerce in acts of appropriation.[31] The difference is, however, that while Baudelaire sought to identify the possibility of extracting transcendent experiences from worldly pleasures, Ellis represents Richard's taste in terms that refuse to surrender a sense of their materiality. Everything Richard wears, from his shoes to his sunglasses, is branded. He clothes himself in a way that emphasises the commodified nature of both his appearance and, by implication, his culture.

Thus, instead of providing protection from the degrading impact of an increasingly commercialised society, these gestures function as registers of the connections between personal preferences and commodification. Unlike Baudelaire, who praises the dandy's 'air of coldness which comes from an unshakeable determination not to be moved' and the way in which 'dandyism borders upon the spiritual and stoical', Ellis offers a portrait grounded on the material.[32] Ellis's character has immersed himself in late capitalism's commodified stream to the point where he simply allows a vast range of experiences to flow through him. This impression is strengthened by Ellis's style which, in a characteristic way, relies on a language centred around commercial labels. Instead of describing colour and appearance, he simply utilises the maker's name and provides a list that includes references to 'Wayfarers', 'Converse' and 'Jack Daniel's'. Where the decadent style looks to heighten the sense of artificiality through the use of elaborate and unusual language, Ellis's style seems brutally unelaborate and referential, firmly rooted in the everyday currency of the brand name. The consequence is that instead of developing a look that stands apart from mainstream codes, Richard seems to reflect them.

This contrast between blank fiction and nineteenth-century decadence can be interpreted by returning to this discussion's sense of the way in which late capitalism differs from monopoly capitalism and considering the influence these contrasting types of economic organisation have on the cultures of these different epochs. The argument revolves, once again, around Mandel's reading of late capitalism as a period of intensified commodification in which the influence of the commodity penetrates into previously uncommercialised spheres. The suggestion is that *The Rules of Attraction* registers these conditions in a narrative that is littered with references to commodities and propelled by textual strategies that mimic the processes of commodification. *The Rules of Attraction*'s repeated emphasis on the relationship between its decadent themes and commercialism appears to represent a type of decadence that seems particularly well-suited to the late capitalist period, one in which the tensions between autonomous pleasures and commodification have disappeared, leaving only consumer based pleasures in their place.

Thinking about the contrast between contemporary capitalism and the economic conditions at the end of the nineteenth century adds weight to this position. As Hobsbawm suggests, the capitalist economy during this period became steadily more global as 'it extended its operations to ever more remote parts of the globe and transformed all areas ever more profoundly'.[33] Unlike the intensely commercialised terrains of late capitalism, the environment Hobsbawm describes is one in which the distinction between commodified and uncommodified spheres still appeared to exist. These conditions, though under serious threat during this period, can thus be linked to the decadent project of the late nineteenth-century writers, a project that could still cling to the possibility of achieving a state untouched by the economic imperatives of the monopoly capitalist period. In contrast, late capitalism is characterised by the absence of uncommodified spheres. Ellis's repeated emphasis on the way in which decadent energies are linked to commodification can, in these terms, be identified with this contemporary situation.

Further reflections on the implications raised by blank fiction's decadent sensibility can be developed by considering Douglas Coupland's *Generation X* (1992), a narrative that describes the indolent routines of a group of 'slackers' who have rejected traditional careers in favour of part-time bar work and a life in Palm Springs. The lack of ambition displayed by the text's three central figures, Dag, Andy and Claire, their contempt for what they see as the 'rat race' and their quest for subtle, sensuous and existential pleasures gives the text a decadent feel. In a project that seems to have a stronger relationship with the work of nineteenth-century *fin de siècle* writers than Ellis's texts, Coupland describes the experiences of individuals who, in response to what they regard as the alienating materialism of the modern world, try to withdraw from it and find a space untouched by its seemingly degraded influence. As far as Coupland's characters are concerned,

> We arrived here speckled in sores ... our systems had stopped working, jammed with the odor of copy machines, Wite-Out, the smell of bond paper, and the endless stress of pointless jobs done grudgingly to little applause. We had compulsions that made us confuse shopping with creativity ... But now we live here in the desert, things are much, *much* better.[34]

This collective response identifies the desert as a place where these individuals can escape from the mundanity and meaninglessness of clerical employment and the numbing impact of consumerism. The desert thus takes on a romantic significance and becomes, in their imaginations, a place set apart from the degrading commercial pressures of everyday experience. Where William Wordsworth, at the start of *The Prelude* (1805), rejected the city, 'the prison where he hath been long immured', in favour of a pastoral environment in which he could receive the 'blessing of the gentle breeze,' Coupland has one of his characters explain how 'he came down here to breathe the dust and walk with the dogs – look at a rock or a cactus and ... try to read the letter inside me'.[35] The desert provides a seemingly uncontaminated environment, a place where economic imperatives have no influence, a space in which a kind of unalienated self-knowledge can be developed. As far as they are concerned, things 'are much, *much* better' in the desert.

The problem is, however, that the desert is not quite as uncommercialised as Coupland's descriptions suggest with the consequence being that the epiphanic moments experienced in this seemingly natural environment are inevitably debased and compromised. As Duncan Webster suggests in *Looka Yonder!*, the representation of the natural environment in contemporary American fiction very often involves the depiction of a space that is 'neither the fields nor the city, but the blurred space in between ... the wheat field glimpsed from the car ... the wide interurban landscape of diners, billboards, barns and buildings seen in the distance'.[36] This impression is supported by the representation of the natural world in *Generation X* which often sees nature merged with the artificial, not cordoned off from it. In one section Andy, Coupland's principle narrator, describes his feelings as he watches the sun coming up:

I sit on the front linai of my rented bungalow ... smelling the cinnamon nighttime pong of the snap dragons and the efficient whiffs of swimming pool chlorine that drift in from the courtyard while I wait for dawn.

nature – commercial undertones.

I look east over the San Andreas fault that lies down the middle of the valley like a piece of overcooked meat. Soon enough the sun will explode over the fault and into my day like a line of Vegas showgirls bursting over the stage.[37]

In a scene that again echoes Wordsworth's *The Prelude* and, in particular, the poet's experiences on the summit of Mount Snowdon, Coupland produces a description that seems to articulate a genuine sense of reverence for the natural world. This impression is disturbed, however, by the constant interruptions of synthetic phenomena. Not only does Andy remain firmly fenced within the artificial surroundings of his bungalow, but he also finds that unnatural elements continually intrude and disrupt his reverie. Though he is able to detect the scent of the snap dragons, this sensation is cancelled out by the chemical 'whiffs' from the surrounding swimming pools, a smell that contaminates the purity of his epiphanic confrontation with nature.

Further emphasis on the significance of artificiality in this scene is provided by his language and by the way he describes the arrival of the sun in terms that have more to do with the commercialised glamour of America's commodified culture than an epiphanic experience. The comparison he draws between the sun and 'the line of Vegas showgirls' develops a sense of the way in which synthetic, urban experiences take precedence over the natural. This environment is not some kind of untouched, romantic Eden, but a space that has, like so many others, been incorporated into America's commercial structures. Even the San Andreas fault is, to an extent, urbanised in Andy's imagination, a geographical feature that he describes, not as some kind of raw, natural phenomena, but as something tamed and domesticated like 'a piece of overcooked meat'.

This contradiction between the text's romantic, escapist desires and its sense of the urban and the commercial finds further expression in the section entitled 'Grow Flowers':

Years ago, after I first started to make a bit of money, I used to go to the local garden store and purchase fifty-two daffodil bulbs. Shortly thereafter I would go into my parent's backyard with a deck of fifty-two wax coated playing cards and hurl the cards across the lawn. Wherever a card fell, I would plant one of the bulbs. Of course I could just have tossed the bulbs themselves, but the point of the matter is, I *didn't*. Planting bulbs this way creates a very natural spray effect – the same silent algorithms that dictate the torque in a flock of sparrows or the gnarl of a piece of driftwood also dictate success in this formal matter too. And come spring, after the daffodil and the narcissi have spoken their delicate little haiku to the world and spilled their cold gentle scent, their crinkly beige onion paper remnants inform us that summer will soon be here and that it is now time to mow the lawn.[38]

It is easy to identify parallels between the concern for sensory pleasure described in this passage and the kind of preoccupations that typified not only Wordsworth's reverence for the natural world, but also the refined sensual experiences favoured by nineteenth-century decadents. Des Esseintes's 'excessive fondness for flowers' is one obvious reference point, a comparison that is supported by the suggestion that the narrator, like Des Esseintes, has fetishised particular products and practices and become obsessed with minute details like the 'fifty-two wax coated playing cards'.[39] The first line, however, reveals a contrast between *Generation X* and the decadent strains of *Against Nature*. Where Huysmans conceals the economic relations that sustain his protagonist's activities, Coupland, by including the phrase 'years ago, after I first started to make a bit of money', discloses the way in which Andy's sensory pleasures depend upon financial foundations. *Generation X* nakedly admits that it purchases its pleasures from the garden centre. In the late capitalist period, this blank novel suggests, even the simplest sensations have a price.

The point raised by these reflections on the fundamentally commercial nature of the decadent experiences described in *Generation X* is that they are offered against the background of the text's overwhelming antagonism towards the commercialism of contemporary American culture. In moments that are very obviously contradicted by the kind of commodified sensations described in Andy's descriptions of the daffodils and his vision of the rising sun, the text offers a rigorously anti-materialistic ethic. Using slogans like 'purchased experiences don't count' and condemning what are described as 'fake yuppie experiences that you ... [have] to spend money on', the narrative appears determined to distance itself from the commercial realm.[40] What is particularly puzzling about this intention is that it is not just opposed by the very obviously commodified nature of the epiphanic moments detailed in the narrative, but that the narrative should be so unaware of this central contradiction. Unable to recognise the commercialised nature of the types of sensations it celebrates, the novel develops a sensibility that seems to be strikingly at odds with the kind of environment in which this sensibility is supposed to operate. Thus the text creates significant tensions between the illusion of transcendence and these inescapable material realities. These tensions can be explored in greater detail by considering the foundations upon which *Generation X*'s paradoxical anti-materialism is based.

The key reference for any discussion of the culture associated with *Generation X* is Richard Linklater's film *Slacker* (1992). This film, along with Coupland's novel, provides not only the terminology but also the framework for definitions of this hazy youth culture. In *Slacker,* Linklater's camera skims around the town of Austin describing the experiences of a large number of under-employed white youths in a suitably tangled and directionless series of loosely interrelated narratives.[41] Like *Generation X*, the characters seem intent on rejecting traditional roles and determined to find alternative paths, preferably paths that offer the least resistance and enable them to satisfy their obscure and often indulgent desires.[42] Indolence is central to the anti-establishment philosophy of this 'slacker culture', a culture which develops, as Linklater suggests, from the actions of individuals

> who might look like the left-behinds of society, but are actually one step ahead, rejecting most of society and the social hierarchy before it rejects them. The dictionary defines slackers as people who evade duties and responsibilities.

A more modern notion would be people who are ultimately being responsible to themselves and not wasting their time in a realm of activity that has nothing to do with who they are or what they might ultimately be striving for.[43]

Central to Linklater's argument is a desire to rebel against or reject accepted norms and an attempt to establish a culture focused around the act of 'rejecting most of society', a process that the slackers feel enables them to get 'one step ahead'. The traditional constraints of professional life and familial responsibility are thus represented as something to be avoided at all costs. In these terms, Linklater echoes the feelings of the characters in *Generation X* who claim to have found a better world by exchanging office work for a lifestyle that enables them to satisfy their romantic notions.

With this rebellion in mind, Douglas Rushcoff insists that the slacker sensibility requires a 'conscious effort to avoid engaging in anything that requires descent into the rat-race or consumerist angst, a neo-Buddhism where attachments of any kind break the awareness so valuable to surfers of a consumer culture'.[44] There is, however, a conflict between the yearning for a 'neo-Buddhism' and the parallel urge to embrace elements of consumer culture and 'surf' across the top of it. In the same way that Ellis's *Less Than Zero* finds itself caught between condemning the degrading effects of consumerism and celebrating many of its more extreme manifestations, slacker culture seems to adopt an equally paradoxical position in which it both revels in the matrix of the popular and, at the same time, tries to distance itself from it.

The insight into the contradictory character of positions articulated by slacker culture can be given more substance by thinking about the way in which Rushcoff develops the sense of slacking as a kind of lifestyle choice. The point is that these choices constitute the slacker's most obvious luxury, a range of options that define them as privileged despite their apparent contempt for privilege and their seemingly low-rent lifestyles. In remarks made about his second film *Dazed and Confused* (1994), Linklater observes that he is presenting characters that 'would be smart enough to go to grad school but ... definitely didn't want to go'.[45] In these comments he emphasises the importance of choice and is at pains to point out that it is not lack of ability nor the absence of necessary funds that dictate terms for these people, but the simple act of choosing. The problem is, however, that while this sense of choice makes their actions seem more deliberate, it also gives them a luxurious complexion. These are individuals who are able to make certain kinds of choices, decisions that seem more like expressions of privilege than anti-materialist gestures.

What makes these reflections seem particularly interesting is not only that they undermine the slacker's identification with a rebellious counter-cultural attitude fired by what *they* see as 'an unprecedented moral and intellectual courage to confront issues rather than cower before them', but also that they reveal the presence of a world-view that seems to articulate a set of expectations that are very obviously those of middle-class aspirants.[46] This world view is particularly apparent in *Generation X*, a novel in which the characters continually emphasise this lack of opportunity and the sense of bitterness it inspires. In one scene Andy, while in the act of quitting his job, attacks his employer's attitudes, saying

> Do you really think we *enjoy* hearing about your million dollar home when we can barely afford to eat Kraft Dinner sandwiches in our own grimy little shoeboxes and we're pushing *thirty*? A home you won in a genetic lottery, I might add, sheerly by dint of your having been born at the right time in history.[47]

This resentment provides a counter-perspective on the novel's insistence that the slacker way of life is taken up as a conscious choice and empowered by attitudes in which the 'nonownership of material goods [is] flaunted as a token of moral and intellectual superiority'.[48] This is a novel that attempts to celebrate the actions of characters who argue that 'you can either have a house or a life ... I'm having a *life*', but in fact ends up portraying characters who would like to own houses if they could, but can't afford to.[49] Unable to pay for mortgages, they are forced to derive some kind of 'moral and intellectual superiority' from what is, in effect, a compulsory anti-materialism.

The compromised positions expressed by Coupland's characters thus contrast sharply with the kind of decadent experiences portrayed in Baudelaire, Huysmans and Wilde. Nowhere is *Generation X*'s co-option more obvious than in its style which seems always to incline towards the mundane. In terms that shadow Spivak's reading of the decadent style, Matei Calinescu argues that decadent writing 'places such an emphasis on details that the normal relationship of a work's parts to its whole is destroyed, the work disintegrating into a multitude of overwrought fragments'.[50] In contrast, Coupland's style seems to function on a principle that privileges the simple over the elaborate and the mundane over the exotic. His approach is 'underwrought', not 'overwrought', with his glib turn of phrase and continual emphasis on slogans making the text both easy to digest and setting it apart from what Calinescu regards as the decadent style's characteristic use of the awkward, the unusual and the 'overwrought fragment'. Coupland writes in catch-phrases, a method that is graphically illustrated in the sound-bites that pattern the margins of his text. Slogans like 'Bench Press your IQ' and 'You Must Choose Between Pain and Drudgery' seem to owe more to commercial writing than decadent experiments.[51] His use of different styles of type adds to this impression. Instead of separating the text from the flow of everyday life, these phrases seem to trammel it, guiding it along a familiar road lined with these intellectual billboards. As Julia Evans suggests in her review of Coupland's second novel *Shampoo Planet* (1993), his writing darts 'from one conceptual snack to the next ... characters rattle out like matchboxes on a conveyor belt. Concerns are gestured at. Still waters run shallow.'[52]

Generation X's apparent decadence thus seems based on very narrow and limited kinds of indulgence. This is a constrained decadence barely worthy of the name. The contradictions in the novel's escapist, rebellious ethos have been exposed in a way that offers a problematic insight into the close affinities between contemporary culture and the slacker's critique of that culture. In one sense this underlines the problems facing projects that attempt to find some kind of critical space outside the boundaries of contemporary culture, while in another it offers an insight into the diluted decadence of the slackers, a world-view which may promise to produce an antidote to conditions in the late twentieth century, but in reality only offers another version of those conditions.

It is important to recognise, however, that in criticising slacker culture in this way there is a chance that it is actually being taken more seriously than it either deserves to be or intends to be. It is, perhaps, unfair, to question its inconsistencies and theoretical flaws, when in fact its philosophical ambitions are strictly limited. Slacking for both Coupland and Linklater is more of a zeitgeist than a philosophy, based on emotion and instinct rather than reason and analysis. When read in this way it becomes possible to interpret its contradictions not as fatal flaws, but as elements that offer a perspective on the relationship between these kinds of narratives and their contemporary contexts. In, for example, the tensions between *Generation X*'s anti-materialist stance and the thoroughly commodified nature of so many of the events it describes lies a relationship that can be fitted in alongside the concerns that have dominated this discussion, offering as they do further insights into the links between these fictions and material conditions in contemporary America. The commodified decadence described in *Generation X* offers another potent image of the intensively commercialised culture that has been identified as one of the defining features of late capitalism.

The restricted, commodified and thoroughly cosseted pleasures represented in Coupland's *Generation X* are not, however, the only kinds of decadence portrayed in blank fiction. In a text like Gary Indiana's *Horse Crazy* (1989), for example, a more extreme and problematic vision of indulgence is offered, one that creates an uncomfortable, self-destructive mood by producing a detailed description of the effects of heroin use. Where narratives like *Generation X* and *Slacker* either avoid the subject of drugs altogether or restrict their focus to the effects of marijuana, Indiana confronts the much more troubling kinds of pleasure offered by heroin in his account of the platonic relationship between the narrator, a struggling New York writer and Gregory, a heroin-addicted photographer.

The novel's representation of heroin offers a reflection on a decadence that, unlike so many of the pleasures depicted in *Generation X*, is fundamentally self-destructive. It can, as a result, be linked much more convincingly to the nihilism of nineteenth-century *fin de siècle* writers. In the same way that they saw 'no possibility at all in reforming society' and 'set about distancing themselves from it', Indiana's representation of the late twentieth-century heroin addict offers a similarly pessimistic vision, one made even more so by the links the text establishes between intravenous drug-use and HIV and AIDS.[53] In *Horse Crazy*, Indiana's narrator describes how 'half the addicts in New York have HIV infection from needle-sharing, and of course the addict knows all this but can't do anything about it because it's the drug that makes all the decisions'.[54] The heroin addicts he describes willingly absolve themselves of all responsibility and embrace pleasures that they know could kill them. In this respect they seem determined to put their own indulgences above everything else, even their own lives. For the heroin user, like the nineteenth-century decadent, the future is meaningless and the only satisfaction lies in immediate indulgence, no matter what the cost.

The decadent tone of Indiana's representation of heroin use is heightened through the emphasis he places on the relationships between pleasure and mortality. In one section he writes of HIV infection in more specific terms, suggesting that 'you would naturally connect your most vivid memory of pleasure to infection and death because the others weren't remotely worth getting sick from'.[55] This destructive indulgence identifies these drug users as individuals who have become involved in a nihilistic complex of sensations that link pleasure to dissolution and death. These addicts express an overwhelming desire to seek alternative kinds of experience and are, as Stephen Perrin argues, individuals whose activities form the 'ultimate expression of radical social and emotional alienation'.[56] Indiana's representations of the heroin user as a marginalised, decadent outsider thus offer an alternative to the sanitised indulgences described in *Generation X*. Like a nineteenth-century decadent, the heroin addict is seeking a space separate from society, a space where relief from its pressures and disillusionment with its norms can be freely expressed. The heroin addict seems to achieve a kind of decadent autonomy, a liberation that is not without its destructive consequences, but one that, nevertheless, appears to provide the desired sequestration.

This autonomy is not, however, as uncomplicated or complete as this argument suggests for it is reliant on an artificial stimulus that inevitably compromises the user's pleasure. In David Wojnarowicz's *Close to the Knives* (1991), an autobiographical novel about drug use, hustling, AIDS-related illness and death, the narrator suggests that the manufactured nature of his drug-induced experiences tends to reduce their liberating effects. Wojnarowicz's narrator explains his feelings in the following terms:

> There's a slow sensation of that type coming into the body, from the temples to the abdomen to the calves, and riding with it in waves, spurred on by containers of coffee, into the marvelousness of light and motion and figures coasting along the streets. Yet somehow that feeling of beauty that comes riding off each surface and movement around me always has a slight trace of falseness about it, a slight sense of regret, felt at the occurring knowledge that it's a substance flowing in my veins.[57]

The fact that he has ingested a 'substance' takes the edge off his experience of the 'marvelousness of light' and gives it this 'slight trace of falseness'. His perspective can be tied to a more concrete reading of 'substance', a word that gestures towards a greater sense of the links between these experiences and the material realities of the society they are supposed to be freeing him from. The drug user is tied to social and economic relations in particular ways through the material function of the drug as a 'substance', a product and, by implication, a commodity. The 'conciliatory gleam' Benjamin saw in Baudelaire's decadent images of nineteenth-century Paris is thus echoed in the way writers like Wojnarowicz and Indiana describe drug use. The difference is, however, that this conciliating, elevating process unravels as it becomes apparent that drug taking works ultimately to re-establish a sense of materiality.

These processes are dramatised in even clearer terms in the title story from Evelyn Lau's collection *Fresh Girls* (1994). 'Fresh girls', a typically blank and unimpassioned description of life in a brothel, includes a scene in which the narrator accepts a shot of heroin from her pimp:

> She's tearing open the package and chattering, but I hardly notice, my arm is turned up on the couch, Mark is telling me to pump my hand and saying, 'Good, good girl, that's it, there it is,' and I'm leaning back against the back of the sofa real fast, tasting the taste of it come up in my throat, like silver or copper or one of those metals, and that silvered feeling all along the back of my neck where it'll hurt next morning.[58]

Clear reflections of *Generation X*'s emphasis on the commercial dimensions of the pleasure derived from growing flowers can be seen in this section's representation of heroin use. In detailing the opening of 'the package' Lau, like Coupland, works to foreground the commodified origins of this particular experience, with the wrapper marking heroin as a specific kind of commercial indulgence. The narrator develops this position through a description that employs a language coloured by financial associations. Heroin gives her 'that silvered feeling' and through the process of comparing the taste of the heroin rush to 'silver or copper or one of those metals' she establishes a sense of the commercial character of her experiences. In nineteenth-century *fin de siècle* writing, or even in the apocalyptic heroin rushes described in Indiana's *Horse Crazy*, the onset of the pleasurable sensation would be the moment in which the base material world would be left behind. Lau's blank writing offers a different perspective, telling a story in which the sensory experience draws the narrator into an intense, heroin-induced contemplation of the commodified character of her chosen indulgence. Like the individuals in Wojnarowicz's work, Lau's narrator recognises the extent to which her pleasures are dependent upon particular substances, a realisation that inevitably diminishes her euphoria and grounds these potentially transcendent experiences in specific kinds of material relations.

Instead of deriving pleasure through commodities, 'Fresh girls' describes a situation in which pleasure and commodities are experienced as one and the same thing. Central to the text's representation of the extent of the commercial influence is its depiction of intravenous drug use which captures, in the image of the needle piercing the skin, penetrating the body's limits and introducing the product into the bloodstream, a sense of the commodifying process's invasive power. It is possible to develop these ideas by considering the way they reflect on the text's wider thematic interest in prostitution. Connections between the symbolic representation of economic encroachment into the human frame through narcotics and prostitution's commercialisation of the body are clearly apparent and establish a wider sense of the text's anxieties about the influence of commodification.

The economic relations symbolised in drug use are thus grounded on the status of drugs as commodities. The pleasures derived through them are, inevitably, commodified. Nowhere are these relationships more apparent than in the representations of the drug dealer. As William Burroughs argues, junk is the 'ultimate commodity'.[59] The dealers have captive markets of individuals addicted to their wares, desperate for the product. This is true not only of heroin, but of other narcotics as well. As *Iced* (1993), Ray Shell's novel about crack addiction, shows, the need to acquire the addictive drug is all consuming. Shell tells the story of Cornelius's decline into addiction as he exchanges the pleasures of his entrepreneurial success in the music business for the satisfactions of the crack pipe. What makes this transformation interesting is the way the novel develops a sense of the similarities between the commercial world of business and the dedicated labour of the addict. Both, in Shell's terms, are kinds of work. As Cornelius observes, 'the pipe is a grim-hard-task-master. It demands total devotion from its slaves.'[60] Employed in the service of this 'task-master', Cornelius finds himself labouring to acquire the product. For him, 'money is only important as the material that grants ... [me] the object. The pipe.'[61] If Cornelius originally rejected his business success in favour of the sensual pleasures of crack, he soon finds that his pleasure has become business once more as he sets to work in search of the rewards of crack.

A commercial network of relationships once again dominate the representations of pleasure. In *Iced* business and pleasure are one and the same thing. Cornelius works for his draconian master like some nineteenth-century factory worker, labouring constantly to satisfy the demands of this all-consuming system. As was the case in the writing of Lau and Wojnarowicz, the decadent autonomy of the drug user is cancelled out by the material relations generated by his or her dedication to the product. Pleasure is commodified in a series of representations that offer a depressingly familiar sense of the ways in which commercial interests colonise these experiences. In this way, these writers can be seen to be trying to emulate the gestures of nineteenth-century *fin de siècle* writers and attempting to use sensuality and indulgence as a way of casting a 'conciliatory gleam' over normative conditions in the late twentieth century. In the effort to escape, however, they simply reinscribe their beholdenment to those norms. These texts thus offer a vision of a commercial culture that has the power to incorporate and disarm the gestures intended to provide some relief from it.

This representation of drug use as a kind of failed decadence is not, however, the only way drugs are represented in fictions of this kind. Where writers like Lau, Shell and Indiana use drugs as a way of signalling a desire, albeit a futile one, for some kind of freedom or autonomy, other blank fictions use drugs as a symbol of identification rather than rebellion. The use of cocaine, in particular, isn't offered as a gesture that signals deviancy nor as an act intended to cut the user off from the material realities of everyday life, but as an activity that reconfirms the user's place in establishment culture and underlines that individual's status and success. Cocaine, unlike heroin or crack, is deployed as the sign of those who want to drop in rather than drop out. In, for example, *American Psycho*, cocaine is just one of the many commodities that Ellis's wealthy protagonist indulges in, a pleasure that seems to complement his expensive clothes and extravagant tastes. For Bateman cocaine use provides what is, quite simply, just another excuse to consume conspicuously. In a text of this kind there is a very strong equation between success and cocaine use. Cocaine is a drug that is seen to improve efficiency. As Freud insisted its 'stimulative effect ... is vouched beyond any doubt'.[62] In this respect it seems to provide the perfect narcotic for a figure like Patrick Bateman. It is a drug that both underlines his success and increases his sense of power. Where figures in other blank novels take drugs in order to satisfy a decadent desire for liberation, Bateman takes drugs as a way of sharpening his murderous grip on the world.

A similar situation can be found in the novels of Jay McInerney. In *Bright Lights, Big City,* a novel that describes the decline of a promising young publisher, McInerney has his narrator use cocaine as a way of boosting his flagging self-confidence. When, for example, he finds himself alone in a nightclub having been deserted by his friends and realising that there is little chance of meeting anybody to replace his long-gone girlfriend, all he needs to do is 'remember the Bolivian Marching Powder' to appreciate that he is 'not down yet'.[63] Cocaine not only helps him to overcome this self-doubt, but also seems to make him more attractive. Encountering an uninterested single woman, he manages to stimulate her not by talking to her but by giving her drugs, observing that after 'a couple of spoons, she seems to like ... [him] just fine'.[64]

The images of cocaine use in McInerney's *Brightness Falls* work in similar terms, representations that are strengthened by the contrast the novel establishes between cocaine and heroin: where cocaine stimulates, heroin sedates. In *Brightness Falls* the narrative is based on the tensions between Russell, the ambitious professional and Jeff, the hedonistic writer. Throughout the text the life of the cocaine-using publisher is constantly privileged over that of the heroin-addicted artist. Jeff's death from AIDS at the end of the novel provides the final statement on their friendship, a relationship that ends with Jeff falling into decadent self-destruction, while Russell remains alive and intent on restoring his fortunes. Within the symbolism generated by the novel's representations of narcotics the message appears to be that while cocaine use has its problems they can be overcome. The practical, competent cocaine user will not have his or her life destroyed. Heroin, on the other hand, is a drug for those who are doomed to failure. It may be a drug for those who are more artistically gifted, but its creative potential is cancelled out by its negative effects. That

McInerney should 'punish' Jeff's indulgence with AIDS only serves to underline the ultimately conservative position adopted by the text. In *Brightness Falls*, those who stray too far into the excesses symbolised by heroin addiction will suffer the apparently deserved consequences, while those who drift into what are seen to be the relatively safe indulgences of cocaine use will be able to return chastened to the fold.

The straightforward, almost moralistic images of drugs offered in McInerney's work and the use of drugs as a status symbol in *American Psycho* seem to set these texts apart from the kinds of images offered by Lau, Indiana, Wojnarowicz and Shell. In their writing drug use seems much more decadent and the yearning for pleasure linked to a general desire to reject or negate society. This contrast is, however, not as wide as it first appears. The commercial dimensions of drug use seem to tie these decadent energies to mainstream culture and even in texts where the use of drugs is used as an emblem of the desire for autonomy, integration inevitably results. The kind of wilful conformism represented by Ellis is thus reflected in texts that find themselves offering images of co-option in moments intended to signal their rejection of the mainstream. Whether the intention is to rebel or to conform, drug use seems in all of these novels to symbolise a world in which recuperative energies dominate. Drug use and commercialism are seen to be indistinguishable, a relationship that emphasises the extent and influence of commodification in contemporary society.

Though commodified in this way, there is still one sense in which the depiction of drug use in Lau, Shell, Wojnarowicz and Indiana can be seen to problematise this vision of integration. In their blank destructive images of nihilistic pleasure lurk disturbing energies that generate an uneasy, unsettling atmosphere. These excesses, like those described in other blank novels, exceed regulation. The narratives might not feel that they can produce a closed, autonomous world free from the taint of material reality, but still, through the deployment of these disquieting images they manage to do more than simply identify with dominant conditions. Their descriptions of economic encroachment into human experiences create an atmosphere of disquiet that generates a disturbing response to these commodifying processes. The representations of these uneasy, excessive pleasures, though deeply engaged in the commodifying mechanisms of late capitalism, thus manage, despite that engagement, to articulate concerns about those processes. As was the case with other blank fictions, disturbing images of destructive pleasure create a problematic vision of the dynamics of late capitalism. Though in some ways these representations speak of that system's dominance, they also produce dynamics which unsettle that hegemony.

Though many of these writers can be seen to echo *fin de siècle* fiction's interest in extreme experiences and pleasures, the transitory moments of release experienced in nineteenth-century decadent texts are only momentarily reflected in blank fiction. This key difference can be interpreted by considering the way in which nineteenth-century decadence sees a resistance to commodification that blank fiction can not share. Though decadent writing's strategy is largely futile, there is a sense in which it achieves transitory moments of pure, uncommodified pleasure. This is not the case, however, with blank fiction. Where pleasure in decadent writing offers the promise of temporary escape, in blank fiction pleasure is explored more in ways that illustrate the extent of commod-ification's encroachment into human experience than to offer any relief from it. As a result these texts produce a detailed vision of the increasingly commodified character of the contemporary world. In this environment even the simplest pleasures are seen to be not made available through consumption, but actually dependent on commodification itself, a dependency that underlines the extent to which decadence and commerce have become interrelated in the late twentieth-century imagination.

7

Blank Fictions

In *New York Fictions*, Peter Brooker suggests that 'at its most extreme, postmodernism ... becomes a celebratory or fatalistic aesthetic, a self-ratifying denial of any effective cultural politics'.[1] His position is that the all-encompassing terms of the postmodernism debate numb and stifle interpretations of late twentieth century culture in ways that lead to a limited and homogenised understanding of the contemporary. Instead of this approach, Brooker argues for perspectives that retain a 'sense of the world of lived social, cultural and economic experience which postmodernism denies'.[2] The analysis of images of consumerism and commodification developed in this discussion of blank fiction echoes the kinds of strategies favoured by Brooker. Though he focuses more on the problematics of ethnicity and subjectivity in late twentieth-century American society, his concerns for a sense of the 'lived ... experience' are satisfied by this discussion's privileging of perspectives that regard culture as a space in which specific social, aesthetic and material forces intersect. Rejecting models that interpret contemporary society as a mysterious and incontestable structure produced by a series of abstract forces in favour of a position that sees late twentieth-century culture as a formation generated by the interaction of individual priorities, industrial imperatives and social experiences, this argument offers a sense of the ways in which contemporary fiction can be read in terms that make these forces visible.

It has been the use of the commodity as the central term that has provided a way of charting these relationships and developing a position that combines a sensitivity to the priorities of individual narratives with a wider sense of context. Using arguments developed from Bourdieu's work to establish an understanding of the complex range of significances articulated by consumerism, these chapters have provided a perspective on the tensions and interrelationships between this particular cultural form and the wider conditions in late twentieth-century America. Rejecting theories of a mysterious, incontestable postmodern sublime, for a position that sees contemporary culture as a formation produced at the intersection of a variety of different forces, this argument attempts to read blank fiction in terms that refuse to surrender to the 'fatalistic, self-ratifying' positions criticised by Brooker. Thus, instead of regarding these aesthetic forms as the mute product of late capitalism's cultural logic, the suggestion is that they can be interpreted as narratives that disclose some of the key dynamics operating in contemporary culture.

Central to this approach has been a close concern for the issues raised by blank fiction itself. These arguments are not offered as an abstract theoretical guide to fiction of this kind, but developed in ways that reflect blank fiction's own obsession with mass culture and mass consumption. Blank fiction's relentless emphasis on brand names, popular culture and commodities, coupled with its detailed descriptions of consumerism, the reifications of violence, decadence and extreme sexuality, provide the boundaries within which this study has been developed. Without these components there would only be theory; with them that theory becomes an argument tailored to the analysis of the specific concerns raised by fiction of this kind. The conclusion is that any reading of blank fiction requires an interpretation of the meaning of commodification, an analysis that both facilitates a contextual understanding of these texts and produces a range of concerns that fit alongside the priorities of the narratives themselves.

Though the emphasis on commodification seems to provide insights into blank fiction, it is apparent that, even at the end of this discussion, a clear definition of this type of writing remains elusive. The preceding chapters have identified a series of thematic connections, but those links are inevitably fluid. A more convincing categorisation can be found by combining an analysis of the content of these fictions with a reading of the blank style, a style that discloses a common set of aesthetic interests and a shared vision. It must be acknowledged, however, that this blank style has been interpreted in different ways and at different times. While it is possible to see similarities between, say, the studied atonality of Lynne Tillman, the indifferent tone of Bret Easton Ellis and the seamless, glassy language of Dennis Cooper, their styles are in no way identical. Though these writers appear to share a number of key aesthetic concerns, it is difficult to group them under one umbrella: there is no 'blank school', nor can they be regarded as part of a coherent literary movement. With this in mind it seems appropriate to suggest that there is not one definitive kind of blank fiction, but a number of different *blank fictions*.

In this context the term 'blank' seems fitting, offering as it does a 'non-definition', a definition that in the very emptiness of the terminology appears to speak of the problematic nature of the attempt to bring these writers together. 'Blank fictions' thus seems suitable, articulating as it does both reservations about the nature of literary categories while, at the same time, offering a label for a loose affiliation of writers who are engaged in the production of a kind of modern fiction that is flat, ambiguous and problematically blank. From this perspective, the neutrality of the term blank fictions seems, paradoxically, to make its categorisations more precise. This neutrality brings other benefits: it has neither positive nor negative connotations. The variety of blank fictions and the wide spread of concerns covered complicate any attempt either to celebrate them unreservedly or criticise them uniformly. This neutrality is particularly important in the context of a discussion that considers such a range of writing. While the specific interpretations of individual texts privilege some of these narratives over others, threaded throughout the argument is the desire to identify the connections that link a range of fictions together in ways that avoid praising some while blaming others.

This approach has specific implications for a study as self-consciously fashionable as this one. The dependence on literary fashion, an almost inevitable feature of criticism focused on contemporary texts, means that it will always be difficult to provide a precise focus on the particular characteristics of these kinds of narrative. In a field where priorities are still waxing and waning, the use of the word 'blank' seems almost to leave the category open, waiting, perhaps, for that blank to be filled by a term that has been weighed, measured and assessed over time and applied with the benefit of hindsight. Though, at this stage, the work of writers like Ellis, Cooper and Tillman seems likely to endure, at least for the time being, other novels considered here, particularly D'Amato's *Beauty* and Coupland's *Generation X*, appear, even now, to be ageing badly. It is appropriate, with these concerns in mind, that while the shape and character of this type of writing still seems mobile and prone to fashionable variation, the space allowed for labelling must, for the time being at least, remain blank. This discussion's dependence on fashion does not, however, devalue its conclusions. On the contrary there seems to be something particularly appealing about producing a fashionable study about fictions that are themselves so intimately concerned with fashion, the vagaries of consumerism and the fluctuations of popular culture.

Though the directions blank fictions might take in the future are unclear, what is certain is that this kind of writing is reaching an expanding audience and becoming a more and more important part of contemporary American culture. Ellis and McInerney have already found themselves a place in the hierarchy of American literature and with long careers still ahead of them they will continue to consolidate their positions. Dennis Cooper's profile is also growing. With his name now established in Europe as well as America and a mythical reputation fuelled by his publishers, style magazines and rumour, his next novel is sure to be his most successful to date and will almost certainly establish him as a major writer on the contemporary American scene. Like Cooper, Evelyn Lau, Susanna Moore, Sapphire and Lynne Tillman are also continuing to write and continuing to receive favourable critical attention. The work of these writers is being supported by an increasing number of new novelists writing in terms that echo and develop the preoccupations of these earlier blank fictions. The increasing reputation of Dale Peck, who followed his first novel *Fucking Martin* with the acclaimed *The Law of Enclosure* (1996), is one example. The success of Jennifer Belle's *Going Down* (1996), a *Slaves of New York*-style journey through New York high-life and low-life is another. Many other recent writers have followed in a similar vein: Sin Soracco's *Edge City*

(1993), Benjamin Weissman's *Dear Dead Person* (1994) and Linda Yablonsky's *The Story of Junk* (1997) are works that suggest that the first generations of blank writers are being supplemented by the arrival of the second and the third.

Interest in one area has, however, declined. The instant success of Coupland's *Generation X* has not been sustained. In response Coupland has moved away from issues raised in his first novel towards work focused on the relationship between individual identities and personal computers. Coupland's trajectory has been shadowed by Douglas Rushcoff whose *The Ecstasy Club* (1997) is set in a 'virtual community' and peopled with the 'screen-agers' who inhabit the world-wide-web. Coupland's slacker-cohort, Richard Linklater, has also moved on from his days as an X-er with his most recent films providing more general commentaries on youth culture. Narratives in the style of *Generation X* and *Slacker* are, however, still being produced. Jeff Gomez's *Our Noise* (1995) is one obvious example, as are the films of Kevin Smith: *Clerks* (1994), *Mallrats* (1995) and *Chasing Amy* (1997). The mainstream success of Cameron Crowe's Hollywood-financed slacker-movie *Singles* (1993), a film that stands as an emblem of the way in which the slacker ethos has been compromised, commercialised and professionalised, does, however, suggest that this particular strand of blank fiction has run its course.

Though this type of writing may be fading from view, there is no doubt that the influence of blank fiction in general is continuing to grow. The publication of Rosa Liksom's Helsinki-based series of blank stories, *One Night Stands* (1993), the emergence of Will Self and Helen Zahavi in Britain and the phenomenal international success of Irvine Welsh's *Trainspotting* (1993) suggest that blank fiction can no longer be regarded as a uniquely American mode. Welsh's writing in particular seems firmly indebted to the concerns that typify American blank fictions and has opened the door for a whole range of new British writing in this vein. The expansion into Europe has been partnered by developments that have seen it find an increasingly secure position in the American cultural mainstream. The success of the sitcom *Friends* is one sign of this consolidation as is the rise of new Hollywood directors like Quentin Tarantino and Robert Roderiguez. Speculation about forthcoming film versions of *American Psycho*, *Frisk* and *In The Cut* adds weight to this suggestion and underlines the extent to which the influence of this kind of writing has grown. No longer can blank fiction be dismissed as the aberrant productions of some marginal group.

In the light of these recent changes it seems that the themes and styles adopted by blank fictions will ultimately find a place at the heart of the American cultural mainstream. This destination seems in many ways fitting, providing as it does a context for a kind of writing that is preoccupied with mass culture and the forces shaping and mediating consumer society. It is, as the preceding chapters have suggested, this emphasis on the commercial that provides the key to understanding these texts. Though blank fictions might seem to lack social content, through these engagements with consumer society they manage to reveal the relationships between their literary concerns and a wider social and material context. Blank fictions' fantasies of consumption are not dreams about the domination of the commodity nor are they visions that reflect its all-colonising power, but fantasies in which the features of late twentieth-century America are traced, disclosed and made intelligible.

Notes

Chapter 1: Reading the Scene

1. Robert Siegle, *Suburban Ambush: Downtown Writing and the Fiction of Insurgency* (Baltimore: Johns Hopkins University Press, 1989), p. 2; Elizabeth Young and Graham Caveney, 'Introduction', in Elizabeth Young and Graham Caveney, *Shopping in Space: Essays on American 'Blank Generation' Fiction* (London: Serpent's Tail, 1992), p. *vii*.
2. cf. Amy Scholder and Ira Silverberg (eds), *High Risk 2: Writings on Sex, Death and Subversion* (London: Serpent's Tail, 1994).
3. cf. Adam Parfrey (ed.), *Apocalypse Culture*, expanded and revised edition (Los Angeles: Feral House, 1990).
4. cf. Douglas Coupland, *Generation X* (London: Abacus, 1992).
5. cf. M. Mark, 'Introduction', in M. Mark (ed.), *Disorderly Conduct: The VLS Fiction Reader* (London: Serpent's Tail, 1991), p. *xii*. He describes this kind of writing as an 'outsider fiction'. See also, Amy Scholder and Ira Silverberg, 'Introduction', in Scholder and Silverberg (eds), *High Risk*, p. *xvii*. They argue that the writers in their collection represent 'some of the most challenging writers from the other side'. See also Siegle, *Suburban Ambush*, p. 2. He describes the 'fiction of insurgency' as a type of writing that is 'making its passage beyond liberationist illusions of free space and unmediated time ... [a] guerrilla campaign against the immanent transformation of American consciousness into a shopping mall'.
6. cf. Steven Connor, *Postmodernist Culture: An Introduction to Theories of the Contemporary* (Oxford: Basil Blackwell, 1989).
7. Linda Hutcheon, *A Poetics of Postmodernism: History, Theory, Fiction* (New York: Routledge, 1988); Fredric Jameson, 'Postmodernism and consumer society', in Hal Foster (ed.), *Postmodern Culture* (London: Pluto Press, 1987), p. 125.
8. Terry Eagleton, *Marxism and Literary Criticism* (London: Methuen, 1976), p. 34.
9. Richard Godden, *Fictions of Capital: The American Novel from James to Mailer* (Cambridge: Cambridge University Press, 1990), p. 7.

10. V.N. Vološinov, *Marxism and the Philosophy of Language*, trans. Ladislav Matejka and I.R. Tutnick (New York: Seminar Press, 1973), p. 18.
11. Ibid., p. 102 (original italics).
12. cf. Michel Aglietta, *A Theory of Capitalist Regulation: The U.S. Experience*, trans. David Fernbach (London: NLB, 1979), p. 181. He argues that the contemporary capitalist system needs to 'guarantee the process of social consumption, without which the regime of intensive accumulation would totally collapse'. See also Alain Touraine, *The Post-Industrial Society: Tomorrow's Social History – Classes, Conflicts and Culture in a Programmed Society*, trans. Leonard Mayhew (London: Wildwood House, 1974), p. 19: 'Information, education and consumption are more closely bound than ever to the realm of production.' See also Daniel Bell, *The Coming of Post-Industrial Society: A Venture in Social Forecasting* (Harmondsworth: Penguin, 1976), p. 117. Bell offers a table detailing 'the general schema of [the] social emphasis on change' which includes an outline of the way commodifying processes effect previously uncommodified spaces like 'education', 'recreation' and 'health'.
13. Ernest Mandel, *Late Capitalism*, trans. Joris de Bres (London: Verso, 1978), p. 388.
14. Ibid., p. 267.
15. Robert D'Amico, 'Desire and the commodity form', in *Telos: A Quarterly Journal of Radical Thought* (Spring 1985), no. 35, p. 93 (original italics).
16. Richard Fox and T.J. Jackson Lears, 'Introduction', in Richard Fox and T.J. Jackson Lears (eds), *The Culture of Consumption: Critical Essays in American History, 1880–1980* (New York: Pantheon, 1983), p. *x*.
17. David Lehman, 'Two divine decadents', in *Newsweek*, 7 September 1987, p. 72.

Chapter 2: Violence

1. cf. Nicci Gerrard, 'Bret and the beast in the corner', in The *Observer*, 16 October 1994, p. 18: 'A lot of people – critics panning his novels, feminists campaigning to have his novels banned – accuse Ellis of shock tactics; of exploiting the so-called "splatter-punk" genre in order to push himself back into the limelight.'
2. Tammy Bruce, 'National Organisation of Women' (1990), quoted in Elizabeth Young, 'The beast in the jungle, the figure in the carpet: Bret Easton Ellis's *American Psycho*', in

Young and Caveney, *Shopping in Space*, p. 86; Roger Rosenblatt, 'Snuff this book', in *The New York Times*, 16 December 1990, p. 3. See also Martin Lee, *Consumer Culture Reborn: The Cultural Politics of Consumption* (London: Routledge, 1993), p. 176. Lee describes its 'literary merit and authorial motivation [as] very questionable indeed'. See also Matthew Tyrnauer, 'Who's afraid of Bret Easton Ellis?', *Vanity Fair* (August 1994), p. 101. He reflects on *'Psycho's* ignominious debut, a time when the Walt Disney Company barred him from the opening of Euro Disney'.

3. cf. Robert Zaller, '*American Psycho*, American censorship and the Dahmer case', in *Revue Français D'Etudes Américaines* (July 1993), no. 57. See also John Walsh, 'Accessories before the fact', in *The Sunday Times*, 21 April 1991, p. 5: '*American Psycho* ... has got the book world in a fine old lather for its depictions of sadistic torture and murder. Feminists call it "a how-to guide to the dismemberment of women" as if murder (even in Manhattan) were a matter of awful knowledge, rather than awful will. Its first publisher decided it was too awful to print. Its current publishers would only print it with cuts ... It has in short turned from a book into a cultural embarrassment, an accessory not to be seen dead with.'

4. Bret Easton Ellis, *American Psycho* (London: Picador, 1991), p. 304.

5. cf. Walsh, 'Accessories before the fact', p. 5: 'Ellis uses the consumerist surface, the *thingness*, of modern American life to satirise its greed, ignorance, complacency and moral bankruptcy. In his murky vision, a skewed and suicidal materialism is the sole currency of his young metropolitans, the only stuff of conversation, the single realm of thought, the measure of personal wealth and social health.'

6. Ellis, *American Psycho*, p. 21.

7. Ibid., p. 113.

8. Ibid., p. 80/81.

9. Ibid., p. 39.

10. Ibid., p. 214–221.

11. Ibid., p. 392.

12. Ibid., p. 200.

13. Ibid., p. 202, p. 206.

14. Ibid., p. 171.

15. Ibid., p. 168.

16. Ibid., p. 343.

17. cf. James O'Connor, *Accumulation Crisis* (New York: Basil Blackwell, 1984), p. 237: 'Reagan ... appealed to individuals to assume the economic initiative and increase economic productivity and cited the responsibility of individuals to

traditional family roles. How ideas of traditional individual autonomy and self-help could be reconciled with corporate and state bureaucratic collection he left unanswered.' See also, Gerrard, 'Bret and the beast in the corner', p. 18: 'My books are transgressive and full of disgust, I guess ... it's to do with a reaction to the Reagan–Thatcher time.'

18. Mark Poster, *The Mode of Information: Poststructuralism and Social Context* (Oxford: Polity Press, 1990), p. 13.

19. Ellis, *American Psycho*, p. 8, p. 11, p. 293.

20. Ibid., p. 265.

21. Ibid., p. 200.

22. Young, 'The beast in the jungle', in Young and Caveney, *Shopping in Space*, p. 120.

23. cf. Walsh, 'Accessories before the fact', p. 5: 'Ellis's most potent thematic conceit is that modern America is a world in which all traces of individuality have been eliminated.'

24. Ellis, *American Psycho*, p. 250, p. 90.

25. This kind of psychological history is often used to 'explain' the behaviour of murders both in fiction and in reality. A classic reading in this vein can be found in Flora Rhita Schrieber, *The Shoemaker: Anatomy of a Psychotic* (London: Allen Lane, 1983), an analysis of the crimes of Joseph Kallinger, a Philadelphia shoemaker. See also Norman Mailer, 'Children of the Pied Piper', in *Vanity Fair* (March 1991), p. 183. Mailer argues that Ellis's failure to supply Bateman with 'enough inner life for us to understand him', is one of the novel's key weaknesses.

26. Young, 'The beast in the jungle', in Young and Caveney, *Shopping in Space*, p. 120.

27. Ralph Waldo Emerson, 'Beauty', in Ralph Waldo Emerson, *The Collected Works of Ralph Waldo Emerson, Volume 1: Native Addresses and Lectures*, ed. Robert Spiller and Alfred Ferguson (Cambridge, Massachusetts: Belknap Press, 1971), p. 15; John Keats, 'Ode on a Grecian urn' (1820), in John Keats, *The Poetical Writings and Other Works of John Keats*, ed. H. Buxton Foreman (New York: Charles Scribner's Sons, 1939), vol. 3, p. 157.

28. Thorstein Veblen, 'The economic theory of woman's dress', in *The Popular Science Monthly* (December 1894), p. 200.

29. Mark Seltzer, *Bodies and Machines* (London: Routledge, 1992), pp. 122/123.

30. cf. Frances Mascia-Lees and Patricia Sharpe (eds), *Tattoo, Torture, Mutilation and Adornment: The Denaturalization of the Body in Culture and Text* (New York: State University of New York Press, 1992).

31. Thorstein Veblen, *The Theory of the Leisure Class: An Economic Study of Institutions* (1899) (London: Unwin Books, 1970), pp. 107/108.
32. Karl Marx, *Capital*, vol. 1, trans. Ben Fowkes (Harmondsworth: Penguin Books, 1976), p. 164.
33. Brian D'Amato, *Beauty* (London: Grafton, 1993), p. 150.
34. Ibid., p. 254.
35. Marx, *Capital*, vol. 1, p. 165.
36. Mike Featherstone, 'The body in consumer culture', in Mike Featherstone, Mike Hepworth and Bryan Turner (eds), *The Body: Social Process and Cultural Theory* (London: Sage, 1991), p. 173.
37. Fredric Jameson, *Postmodernism, or, The Cultural Logic of Late Capitalism* (London: Verso, 1993), p. 36.
38. Fredric Jameson, 'Periodizing the 60s', in Fredric Jameson, *The Ideologies of Theory: Essays 1971 - 1986, Volume 2: The Syntax of History* (London: Routledge, 1988), p. 207.
39. D'Amato, *Beauty*, p. 187, p. 171, p. 198.
40. Ibid., p. 279.
41. W.F. Haug, *Critique of Commodity Aesthetics: Appearance, Sexuality and Advertising in Capitalist Society*, trans. Robert Boch (Cambridge: Polity Press, 1986), p. 17.
42. Ibid., p. 44.
43. Rachel Bowlby, *Just Looking: Consumer Culture in Dreiser, Gissing and Zola* (London: Methuen, 1985), p. 26.
44. cf. Donna Harraway, 'A cyborg manifesto: science, technology and socialist feminism in the late twentieth century', in Donna Harraway, *Simians, Cyborgs and Women: The Reinvention of Nature* (London: Free Association Books, 1991), p. 174: 'There are ... great riches for feminists in explicitly embracing the possibilities inherent in the breakdown of clear distinctions between organism and machine and similar distinctions structuring the Western self.'
45. Dennis Cooper, *Frisk* (London: Serpent's Tail, 1991), p. 106.
46. Roger Clarke, 'Over their dead bodies', in the *Observer*, 25 September 1994, p. 16.
47. Georg Lukács, 'Reification and the consciousness of the proletariat', in Georg Lukács, *History and Class Consciousness: Studies in Marxist Dialectics*, trans. Rodney Livingstone (London: Merlin, 1971), p. 93.
48. Ibid., p. 92.
49. Cooper, *Frisk*, p. 99.
50. Norman O. Brown, *Life Against Death: The Psychoanalytical Meaning of History*, 2nd ed. (Connecticut: Wesleyan University Press, 1985), p. 279.
51. Ibid., p. 295.

52. Ibid., p. 256.
53. Elizabeth Young, 'Death in Disneyland – the work of Dennis Cooper', in Young and Caveney, *Shopping in Space*, p. 260.
54. Elizabeth Young, 'Lost boy', in the *Guardian*, 1 October 1994, p. 29.
55. Dennis Cooper, *Jerk* (San Francisco: Artspace, 1993), p. 50.
56. Ibid., p. 52.
57. Young, 'Lost boy', p. 29; Roland Barthes, *The Pleasure of the Text*, trans. Richard Miller (Oxford: Basil Blackwell, 1990), p. 67.
58. Cooper, *Frisk*, p. 59.
59. Barthes, *The Pleasure of the Text*, p. 67.
60. Cooper, *Frisk*, p. 6, p. 26.

Chapter 3: Sex

1. cf. Michael Shnayerson, 'Women behaving badly', in *Vanity Fair* (February 1997).
2. cf. Jack Gee, 'Madonna: my book isn't porn', in the *Daily Express*, 12 October 1992, p. 1; Phillipa Braidwood, 'Tacky, tawdry and not fit for children', in the *Daily Express*, 22 October 1994, p. 5.
3. Linda Grant, *Sexing the Millennium: A Political History of the Sexual Revolution* (London: HarperCollins, 1993), p. 268.
4. Anna Powell, 'Tripping the dark fantastic', in *Metropolitan* (Winter 1995/6), p. 20, p. 21.
5. Gregory Bredbeck, 'The new queer narrative: intervention and critique', in *Textual Practice* (Winter 1995), no. 9.3, p. 485.
6. Claire Messud, 'Nightmare on Mean Street', in the *Guardian*, 20 April 1996, p. 30.
7. Susanna Moore, *In the Cut* (New York: Alfred A. Knopf, 1995), p. 85.
8. Ibid., pp. 119/120.
9. Ibid., p. 120, p. 121.
10. Gilles Deleuze, 'Coldness and cruelty', in Gilles Deleuze and Leopold von Sacher Masoch, *Masochism* (New York: Zone, 1989), p. 20.
11. cf. Leopold von Sacher Masoch, *Venus in Furs* (1870), in Deleuze and Sacher Masoch, *Masochism*, p. 196: 'She has drawn up a contract by which I am to commit myself on my honour to be her slave for as long as she wishes.' The contracts are of such importance to the novel that the appendix to *Venus in Furs* lists them in full. See, for example, p. 278: 'Your body and your soul too shall belong to me.'
12. Moore, *In the Cut*, p. 121.
13. Ibid., p. 166.

14. Ibid., pp. 176/177.
15. Ibid., p. 169.
16. Joshua Cohen, 'Dying to watch TV: film, postmodernity, systems and DeLillo's *White Noise*', in *Overhere: Reviews in American Studies*, (Summer 1993), vol. 13.1, p. 23.
17. Ibid., p. 23.
18. cf. André Bazin, 'The myth of total cinema', in André Bazin, *What is Cinema?*, vol. 1, ed. and trans. Hugh Gray (California: University of California Press, 1967).
19. Martin Jay, *Downcast Eyes: The Denigration of Vision in Twentieth-Century French Thought* (Berkeley: University of California Press, 1993), p. 459.
20. Laura Mulvey, 'Visual pleasure and narrative cinema', in *Screen* (Autumn 1975), vol. 16.3, p. 14.
21. Jean-Louis Comolli, 'Machines of the visible', in Stephen Heath and Teresa de Lauretis (eds), *The Cinematic Apparatus* (London: Macmillan, 1980), pp. 122/123.
22. Jay, *Downcast Eyes*, p. 429.
23. Guy Debord, *The Society of the Spectacle*, trans. Donald Nicholson-Smith, (New York: Zone, 1994), p. 33.
24. Richard Hell, *Go Now* (London: Fourth Estate, 1996), p. 164.
25. Linda Williams, *Hard Core: Power, Pleasure and the 'Frenzy of the Visible'* (London: Pandora, 1991), p. 106.
26. Ibid, p. 106.
27. Sapphire, 'Trilogy', in Sapphire, *American Dreams* (London: Serpent's Tail, 1994), pp. 46/47.
28. Peter Brooks, *Body Works: Objects of Desire in Modern Narrative* (Cambridge, Massachusetts: Harvard University Press, 1993), p. 274.
29. Jay, *Downcast Eyes*, p. 274.
30. Ibid., p. 216.
31. cf. Roland Barthes, 'The metaphor of the eye', trans. J.A. Underwood, in Georges Bataille, *The Story of the Eye: With Essays by Susan Sontag and Roland Barthes*, trans. Joachim Neugroschel (London: Penguin, 1982).
32. Steven Shaviro, *Passion and Excess: Blanchot, Bataille, and Literary Theory* (Tallahassee: Florida State University Press, 1990), p. 41.
33. Ibid., p. 41.
34. Dennis Cooper, *Try* (London: Serpent's Tail, 1994), pp. 24/25.

Chapter 4: Shopping

1. cf. Craig Owens, *Beyond Recognition: Representation, Power and Culture*, ed. Scott Bryson, Barabara Kruger, Lynne Tillman

and Jane Weinstock, introduced by Simon Watney (Los Angeles: University of California Press, 1992).

2. Brian Wallis, 'An absence of vision and drama', in *Parkett* (1985), vol. 5, pp. 67/68.
3. Lynne Tillman, 'To find words', in Alison Fell (ed.), *Serious Hysterics* (London: Serpent's Tail, 1992), p. 114.
4. Lynne Tillman, 'Weird fucks', in Lynne Tillman, *Absence Makes the Heart* (London: Serpent's Tail, 1990), p. 42.
5. Ibid., p. 33.
6. Elizabeth Young, 'Silence, exile and cunning: the writing of Lynne Tillman', in Young and Caveney, *Shopping in Space*, p. 199.
7. cf. Lynne Tillman, *Motion Sickness* (London: Serpent's Tail, 1991), p. 188, p. 7.
8. Ibid., p. 189.
9. Ibid., p. 159.
10. Ibid., p. 100.
11. John Urry, *The Tourist Gaze: Leisure and Travel in Contemporary Societies* (London: Sage, 1990), p. 3.
12. Tillman, *Motion Sickness*, p. 41.
13. Ibid., p. 36.
14. Ibid., p. 38.
15. Scott Lash and John Urry, *The End of Organized Capitalism* (Cambridge: Polity Press, 1987), p. 6.
16. Mandel, *Late Capitalism*, p. 387.
17. Urry, *The Tourist Gaze*, p. 14.
18. Tillman, *Motion Sickness*, p. 120.
19. cf. John Berger, *Ways of Seeing* (London: BBC and Penguin, 1972), p. 131: 'Publicity as a system only makes a single proposal. It proposes to each of us that we transform ourselves, our lives, by buying something more. This more, it proposes, will make us, in some way richer – even though we will be poorer by having spent our money.'
20. Tillman, *Motion Sickness*, pp. 26/27.
21. Lukács, 'Reification and the consciousness of the proletariat', in Lukács, *History and Class Consciousness*, p. 165.
22. Jameson, *Postmodernism*, p. 36.
23. Ibid., p. 267.
24. Theodore Adorno and Max Horkheimer, *Dialectic of Enlightenment*, trans. John Cumming (London: Verso, 1979), p. 167, p. 85.
25. Jameson, *Postmodernism*, p. x.
26. Fred Pfeil, '"Makin' flippy floppy": postmodernism and the baby-boom PMC', in Fred Pfeil, *Another Tale to Tell: Politics and Narrative in Postmodern Culture* (London: Verso, 1990), p. 98.

27. Stephen Best and Douglas Kellner, *Postmodern Theory: Critical Interrogations* (Houndmills: Macmillan, 1991), p. 167.
28. Mandel, *Late Capitalism*, p. 502.
29. Ibid., p. 502 (original italics).
30. Lukács, 'Reification and the consciousness of the proletariat', in Lukács, *History and Class Consciousness*, p. 169 (original italics); Andrew Feenberg, *Lukács, Marx and the Sources of Critical Theory* (New York: Oxford University Press, 1981), p. 198.
31. John Fiske, *Power Plays, Power Works* (London: Verso, 1993), p. 8.
32. Tillman, *Motion Sickness*, p. 87.
33. Ibid., pp. 87/88.
34. Ibid., pp. 88/89.
35. Ibid., p. 32.
36. Ibid., p. 104.
37. Ibid., p. 93.
38. Ibid., p. 76.
39. Rob Shields, 'The individual, consumption, culture and the fate of community', in Rob Shields (ed.), *Lifestyle Shopping: The Subject of Consumption* (London: Routledge, 1992), p. 99.
40. Kasia Boddy, 'No innocent abroad: the fiction of Lynne Tillman', in *Overhere: Reviews in American Studies* (Summer 1994), vol. 14.1, p. 11.
41. Young, 'Silence, exile and cunning', in Young and Caveney, *Shopping in Space*, p. 208.
42. Jameson, *Postmodernism*, p. 49.
43. Peter Nicholls, 'A conversation with Lynne Tillman', in *Textual Practice* (1995), no. 9.2, p. 276.
44. Lynne Tillman, 'On the road with Madame Realism', in Lynne Tillman, *The Madame Realism Complex* (New York: Semiotext(e), 1992), p. 106.

Chapter 5: Labels

1. A brief list of the directors appropriated by Tarantino would have to include Brian DePalma, John Woo, Alfred Hitchcock, Martin Scorsese and Alex Cox. Traces of the writing of David Mamet, Jim Thompson, Raymond Chandler and Ernest Hemingway can also be found in Tarantino's work. He adds to these allusions by developing self-referential threads between his own works. His films suggest, for example, that Vincent Vega (John Travolta) in *Pulp Fiction* is the brother of *Toothpick* Vic Vega (Michael Madsen) in *Reservoir Dogs*.

2. cf. Patricia Waugh, *Metafiction: The Theory and Practice of Self-Conscious Fiction* (London: Methuen, 1984).
3. Barthes, *The Pleasure of the Text*, p. 36.
4. Hutcheon, *A Poetics of Postmodernism*, p. 127.
5. Julia Kristeva, *Desire in Language: A Semiotic Approach to Literature and Art*, ed. Leon S. Roudiez, trans. Thomas Gora, Alice Jardine and Leon S. Roudiez (Oxford: Basil Blackwell, 1980), p. 83.
6. Jameson, *Postmodernism*, p. 18
7. Bret Easton Ellis, *Less Than Zero* (London: Picador, 1985), pp. 95/96.
8. Elizabeth Young, 'Vacant possession: *Less Than Zero* – a Hollywood hell', in Young and Caveney, *Shopping in Space*, p. 24.
9. F. Scott Fitzgerald, *The Great Gatsby* (1926) (Harmondsworth: Penguin, 1984), p. 72.
10. Tyrnauer, 'Who's afraid of Bret Easton Ellis?', p. 70.
11. Ellis, *Less Than Zero*, p. 140
12. Dick Hebdidge, *Hiding in the Light* (London: Routledge, 1988), p. 157 (original italics).
13. Ibid., p. 178.
14. Ibid., p. 179.
15. Ellis, *Less Than Zero*, p. 12.
16. E. Ann Kaplan, *Rocking Around the Clock: Music Television, Postmodernism and Consumer Culture* (London: Methuen, 1987), p. 29
17. Ellis, *Less Than Zero*, p. 9.
18. cf. Edward Soja, *Postmodern Geographies: The Reassertion of Space and Time in Critical Social Theory* (London: Verso, 1989), p. 246: 'With exquisite irony, contemporary Los Angeles has come to resemble more than ever before a giant agglomerate of theme parks, a life space comprised of Disney World. It is a realm divided into showcases of global village cultures ... all-embracing shopping malls ... corporation sponsored magic kingdoms, high-technology-based experimental communities of tomorrow, attractively packaged places of rest and recreation, all cleverly hiding the buzzing work stations and labour-process which help to keep it together.'
19. Bret Easton Ellis, *The Informers* (London: Picador, 1994), pp. 157/158.
20. Lawrence Grossberg, 'MTV: swinging on the (postmodern) star', in Ian Angus and Sut Jhally (eds), *Cultural Politics in Contemporary America* (New York: Routledge, 1989), p. 254.
21. Todd Gitlin, 'Looking through the screen', in Todd Gitlin (ed.), *Watching Television* (New York: Pantheon, 1986), p. 5 (original italics).

22. Ellis, *Less Than Zero*, p. 104.
23. David Pan, 'Wishing for more', in *Telos: A Quarterly Journal of Critical Thought* (Summer 1988), no. 76, p. 144. See also Peter Freese, 'Bret Easton Ellis, *Less Than Zero*: entropy in the "MTV novel" ?', in Reingard Nishik and Barbara Korte (eds), *Modes of Narrative: Approaches to American, Canadian and British Fiction* (Wurzburg: Konighausen and Neumann, 1990).
24. Ellis, *Less Than Zero*, p. 26, p. 58.
25. cf. Pierre Bourdieu, *La Distinction: Critique Sociale du Jugement* (Paris: Les Editions de Minuit, 1979), pp. 596/597.
26. Lee, *Consumer Culture Reborn*, p. 49.
27. Ellis, *Less Than Zero*, p. 23.
28. Fitzgerald, *The Great Gatsby*, p. 70
29. Ellis, *Less Than Zero*, p. 25; p. 95.
30. Ibid., p. 63.
31. Ibid., p. 38.
32. These slogans appear throughout Ellis's *Less Than Zero*. See for example, p. 9, p. 23, p. 38, p. 95, p. 176.
33. Bret Easton Ellis, *The Rules of Attraction* (London: Picador, 1987), p. 184.
34. Ibid., p. 19, p. 99, p. 100.
35. Tony Bennett, 'Introduction: popular culture and the "turn to Gramsci"', in Tony Bennett, Colin Mercer and Janet Woollacott (eds), *Popular Culture and Social Relations* (Milton Keynes: Open University Press, 1986), p. *xiii*.
36. cf. Jean-Francois Lyotard, *The Postmodern Condition: A Report on Knowledge*, trans. Geoffrey Bennington and Brian Massumi (Manchester: Manchester University Press, 1984), p. 76: 'One listens to reggae, watches a Western, eats McDonald's food for lunch and local cuisine for dinner.' See also Terry Eagleton, 'Capitalism, modernism and postmodernism', in *New Left Review* (July/August 1985), no. 152, p. 72, where Eagleton refers to 'Lyotard's jet-setters'.
37. Best and Kellner, *Postmodern Theory*, p. 188.
38. Duncan Webster, *Looka Yonder! The Imaginary America of Popularist Culture* (London: Comedia, 1988), p. 174.
39. Ellis, *Less Than Zero*, pp. 207/208.
40. Ibid., p. 207.
41. cf. Fitzgerald, *The Great Gatsby*, p. 29.
42. Young and Caveney, 'Introduction', in Young and Caveney, *Shopping in Space*, p. *vii*.
43. Dennis Cooper, *Closer* (London: Serpent's Tail, 1994), p. 3.
44. Ibid., p. 11.
45. Dick Hebdidge, *Subcultures: The Meaning of Style* (London: Routledge, 1988), p. 19.

46. Sadie Plant, *The Most Radical Gesture: The Situationist International in a Postmodern Age* (London: Routledge, 1992), p. 144.
47. Lev Raphael, 'Betrayed by David Bowie', in Lev Raphael, *Dancing on Tisha B'Av* (London: GMP, 1990), p. 99.
48. Ibid., p. 105.
49. Richard Dyer, *Heavenly Bodies: Film Stars and Society* (Houndmills: Macmillan, 1986), p. 10.
50. Ibid., p. 5.
51. Judith Williamson, *Decoding Advertisements* (London: Marion Boyars, 1978), p. 12.
52. Ellis, *The Rules of Attraction*, p. 261.
53. Mark Leyner, *Et Tu, Babe* (London: Flamingo, 1993), p. 24.

Chapter 6: Decadence

1. cf. Parfrey (ed.), *Apocalypse Culture*. Parfrey's collection of articles and documents is intended to offer an image of a culture that is, in his terms, living with (p. 7) 'just a few short ticks to the third millenium'.
2. The term 'endism' is taken from James Atlas, 'What is Fukuyama saying?', in *The New York Times*, 22 October 1989, p. 38.
3. cf. Elaine Showalter, *Sexual Anarchy: Gender and Culture at the Fin de Siècle* (London: Bloomsbury, 1991), p. 18: 'The 1980s and 1990s ... compulsively tell and retell the stories of the 1880s and 1890s.'
4. cf. Ibid., p. 188: 'Syphilis and AIDS have both occupied similar positions at the ends of the nineteenth and twentieth centuries as both diseases seem to be the result of sexual transgression and have generated moral panic.'
5. cf. Ibid., p. 1: 'From urban homelessness to imperial decline ... the last decade of the twentieth-century seems to be repeating the problems, themes and metaphors of the *fin de siècle*.'
6. Stjepan Mestrovic, *The Coming Fin de Siècle: An Application of Durkheim's Sociology to Modernity and Postmodernism* (London: Routledge, 1991), p. 2.
7. cf. Gillian Beer, 'Representing women: re-presenting the past', in Catherine Belsey and Jane Moore (eds), *The Feminist Reader: Essays in Gender and the Politics of Literary Criticism* (Houndmills: Macmillan, 1989), p. 63. See also Sally Ledger and Scott McCracken, 'Introduction', in Sally Ledger and Scott McCracken (eds), *Cultural Politics at the Fin de Siècle* (Cambridge: Cambridge University Press, 1995), p. 3.

8. cf. Matthew Arnold, *Culture and Anarchy* (1869), ed. Samuel Lipman (New Haven: Yale University Press, 1994).

9. This connection between Juvenal and Veblen is made in Patrick Brantlinger, *Bread and Circuses: Theories of Mass Culture and Social Decay* (Ithaca: Cornell University Press, 1983). These ideas are common currency and it is interesting to note that Bob Sipchen in 'Big hitters gun for Hollywood', in the *Guardian*, 13 June 1995, p. 9, quotes Newt Gingrich's remarks that 'we are becoming what the history books tell us Rome was like: mired in decadent self-absorption and lacking virtue'.

10. cf. Decimus Junius Juvenal, 'Satire X' (circa 125), in Decimus Junius Juvenal, *Sixteen Satires Upon the Ancient Harlot*, ed. and trans. Stephen Robinson (Manchester: Carcanet New Press, 1983), pp. 158/159: 'for they who once / Gave commands, fasces, legions everything, now use / Restraint and only for two things wish anxiously: / Bread and the circuses.'

11. Thorstein Veblen, 'Editorial from *The Dial*', 14 June 1919, in Thorstein Veblen, *Essays on Our Changing Order*, ed. Leon Ardzrooni (New York: Viking 1934), p. 450.

12. cf. John Stokes, 'Introduction', in John Stokes (ed.) *Fin de Siècle/Fin de Globe: Fears and Fantasies of the Late Nineteenth Century* (Houndmills: Macmillan, 1992), p. 1: '*Fin de siècle* myths can be particularly compelling (both inhibiting and compelling), because they feed on data in order to confirm fears.'

13. Roger Clarke, 'Scalpel on the soul' in the *Observer*, 27 March 1994, p. 17.

14. Lehman, 'Two divine decadents', p. 72.; Tyrnauer, 'Who's afraid of Bret Easton Ellis?', p. 73.

15. cf. Joris-Karl Huysmans, *Against Nature* (1884), trans. Robert Baldick (Harmondsworth: Penguin, 1966), p. 22: 'A desert hermitage equipped with all modern conveniences, a snugly heated ark on dry land in which he might take refuge from the incessant deluge of human stupidity.'

16. Walter Pater, *The Renaissance: Studies in Art and Literature* (1873), ed. Adam Philips (Oxford: Oxford University Press, 1986), p. 152.

17. Peter Nicholls, *Modernism: A Literary Guide* (London: Macmillan, 1995), pp. 55/56. This argument is based in a reading of a section from Oscar Wilde, *The Picture of Dorian Gray* (1890), in Oscar Wilde, *Plays, Prose Writings and Poems*, introduced by Isobel Murray (London: Dent, 1975), p. 173: 'The style in which it was written was that curious jewelled style, vivid and obscure at once, full of *argot* and of archaisms, of technical expression and elaborate paraphrases.'

18. Gayatri Spivak, 'The decadent style', in *Language and Style* (1974), vol. 7, p. 229.
19. cf. Charles Baudelaire, 'Love of deceit' in Charles Baudelaire, *Les Fleurs du Mal* (1853), trans. Richard Howard (Brighton: Harvester, 1982).
20. The factors considered here and their influence on decadence have been discussed in a number of places. See, for example, Showalter, *Sexual Anarchy*; Ledger and McCracken (eds), *Cultural Politics and the Fin de Siècle*; Mukulas Teich and Roy Porter (eds), *Fin de Siècle and its Legacy* (Cambridge: Cambridge University Press, 1990).
21. Nicholls, *Modernisms*, p. 54: 'The pursuit of artifice is complicit with a violent rejection of sociality.'
22. cf. Eric Hobsbawm, *Industry and Empire* (Harmondsworth: Penguin, 1969), pp. 176/177: 'By 1900 ... the foundations of the modern large scale industry had been laid ... the last major change was the increase in the *scale* of economic enterprise, the concentration of production and ownership, the rise of an economy composed of a handful of great lumps of rock – trusts, monopolies, oligopolies – rather than a large number of pebbles.'
23. Walter Benjamin, *Charles Baudelaire: A Lyric Poet in the Era of High-Capitalism*, trans. Harry Zohn (London: New Left Books, 1973), p. 170.
24. Ibid., p. 105: 'The poet for the first time faces language the way the buyer faces the commodity on the open market.' See also Terry Eagleton, *Walter Benjamin, or, Towards a Revolutionary Criticism* (London: NLB, 1981), p. 25: 'Strolling through the city ... he displays in living motion something of the commodity's self-contradictory form.'
25. Benjamin, *Charles Baudelaire*, p. 58.
26. Ibid., p. 55.
27. Rosalind Williams, *Dream Worlds: Mass Consumption in Late Nineteenth-Century France* (Berkeley: University of California Press, 1982), p. 136.
28. cf. Nicholls, *Modernisms*, p. 63: 'The decadent self was nourished by the pride it took in recognising that its own values were false, a cynical superiority of view which was also, however an acknowledgement of its own powerlessness to make things otherwise.'
29. Ellis, *The Rules of Attraction*. p. 144.
30. Hebdidge, *Subcultures*, p. 88.
31. Ellen Moers, *The Dandy: Brummell to Beerbohm* (London: Secker and Warburg, 1960), p. 283.
32. Charles Baudelaire, 'The painter of modern life' (1863), in Charles Baudelaire, *The Painter of Modern Life and Other Essays*,

ed. and trans. Jonathan Mayne (London: Phaidon, 1964), p. 29, p. 28.

33. Eric Hobsbawm, *The Age of Empire, 1875–1914* (London: Weidenfeld and Nicolson, 1987), p. 41.
34. Coupland, *Generation X*, p. 11.
35. William Wordsworth, *The Prelude* (1805), Book 1, in William Wordsworth, *The Prelude: A Parallel Text*, ed. J.C. Maxwell (London: Penguin, 1988), p. 34; Coupland, *Generation X*, p. 59.
36. Webster, *Looka Yonder!*, p. 127.
37. Coupland, *Generation X*, p. 4.
38. Ibid., p. 129.
39. Huysmans, *Against Nature*, p. 96.
40. Coupland, *Generation X*, p. 87, p. 91.
41. cf. Douglas Rushcoff's introductory remarks to the section on Linklater's *Slacker* in Douglas Rushcoff (ed.), *The GenX Reader* (New York: Ballantine Books, 1994), p. 40: 'Linklater's movie demonstrated, in both form and content, the meandering, painful, but always ironic and amusing slacker lifestyle.'
42. cf. Derek Malcolm, 'Drop-in for drop-outs', in the *Guardian*, 3 December 1992, p. 28: 'Slacker means ... drop-outs from conventional society who are either unemployed or only do just enough work to feed themselves.' See also Cosmo Landesman, 'The aristos of apathy', in the *Guardian*, 3 December 1992, p. 30: 'Who are they? Aristos of apathy, disaffected, downwardly mobile middle-class kids who are part of the yuppie backlash ... slackerdom is less a movement than a state of mind where nerdism meets nihilism.'
43. This quotation comes from Linklater's interview with himself originally published in the *Austin Chronicle*, quoted in Andrew Kopkind, 'Slacking toward Bethlehem', in *Grand Street* (1993), no. 44, p. 179.
44. Douglas Rushcoff, 'Introduction: us by us', in Rushcoff (ed.), *The GenX Reader*, p. 6.
45. Richard Linklater, 'Interview in *bOING! bOING!*', in Rushcoff (ed.), *The GenX Reader*, p. 46.
46. Rushcoff, 'Introduction', in Rushcoff (ed.), *The GenX Reader*, p. 8.
47. Coupland, *Generation X*, p. 21.
48. Ibid., p. 107.
49. Ibid., p. 142.
50. Matei Calinescu, *Faces of Modernity: Avant-Garde, Decadence, Kitsch* (Bloomington: Indiana University Press, 1977), p. 158.
51. Coupland, *Generation X*, p. 90, p. 62.
52. Julia Evans, 'Shampoo Planet', in the *Guardian*, 6 April 1993, p. 28.

53. Thomas Reed Whissen, *The Devil's Advocates: Decadence in Modern Literature* (New York: Greenwood, 1989), p. *xix*.
54. Gary Indiana, *Horse Crazy* (London: Grafton, 1989) p. 134.
55. Ibid., p. 39.
56. Stephen Perrin, 'Chasing the dragon: The junky as 20th century hero', in *Overhere: Reviews in American Studies* (Summer 1993), no. 13.1, p. 111.
57. David Wojnarowicz, *Close to the Knives* (London: Serpent's Tail, 1992), p. 10.
58. Evelyn Lau, 'Fresh girls', in Evelyn Lau, *Fresh Girls* (London: Minerva, 1994), pp. 5/6.
59. cf. William Burroughs, *Junky* (1953) (London: Penguin, 1977).
60. Ray Shell, *Iced* (London: Flamingo, 1993), p. 40.
61. Ibid., p. 69.
62. Sigmund Freud, 'On cocaine', trans. Steven Edminster and Frederick Redlich, in John Strausbaugh and Donald Blaise (eds), *The Drug User: Documents 1840–1960* (New York: Blast Books, 1991), p. 153.
63. Jay McInerney, *Bright Lights, Big City* (London: Flamingo, 1986), p. 5.
64. Ibid., p. 7.

Chapter 7: Blank Fictions

1. Peter Brooker, *New York Fictions: Modernity, Postmodernism and the New Modern* (Essex: Longman, 1996), p. 15.
2. Ibid., p. 15.

Bibliography

Blank Fictions

Cooper, Dennis, *Frisk* (London: Serpent's Tail, 1991).
—— *Wrong* (London: Serpent's Tail, 1992).
—— *Jerk* (San Francisco: Artspace, 1989).
—— *Closer* (London: Serpent's Tail, 1994).
—— *Try* (London: Serpent's Tail, 1994).
Coupland, Douglas, *Generation X* (London: Abacus, 1992).
—— *Shampoo Planet* (London: Simon and Schuster, 1993).
D'Amato, Brian, *Beauty* (London: Grafton, 1993).
Ellis, Bret Easton, *Less Than Zero* (London: Picador, 1985).
—— *The Rules of Attraction* (London: Picador, 1987).
—— *American Psycho* (London: Picador, 1991).
—— *The Informers* (London: Picador,1994).
Hell, Richard, *Go Now* (London: Fourth Estate, 1996).
Indiana, Gary, *Horse Crazy* (London: Grafton, 1989).
Lau, Evelyn, *Fresh Girls* (London: Minerva, 1994).
Leyner, Mark, *Et Tu, Babe* (London: Flamingo, 1993).
Linklater, Richard, *Slacker* (New York: St Martin's Press, 1992).
Janowitz, Tama, *Slaves of New York* (London: Picador, 1987).
McInerney, Jay, *Bright Lights, Big City* (London: Flamingo, 1986).
—— *The Story of My Life* (London: Penguin, 1989).
—— *Brightness Falls* (London: Penguin, 1992).
Moore, Susanna, *In the Cut* (New York: Alfred A. Knopf, 1995).
Raphael, Lev, *Dancing on Tisha B'Av* (London: GMP, 1990).
Sapphire, *American Dreams* (London: Serpent's Tail, 1994).
Scholder, Amy and Silverberg, Ira (eds), *High Risk: An Anthology of Forbidden Writings* (London: Serpent's Tail, 1991).
—— *High Risk 2: Writings on Sex, Death and Subversion* (London: Serpent's Tail, 1994).
Shell, Ray, *Iced* (London: Flamingo, 1993).
Sontag, Susan, *The Way We Live Now* (London: Cape, 1986).
Tillman, Lynne, *Haunted Houses* (New York: Poseidon Press, 1987).
—— *Absence Makes the Heart* (London: Serpent's Tail, 1990).
—— *Motion Sickness* (London: Serpent's Tail, 1991).
—— *The Madame Realism Complex* (New York: Semiotext(e), 1992).
—— *Cast in Doubt* (London: Serpent's Tail, 1992).

Wojnarowicz, David, *Close to the Knives* (London: Serpent's Tail, 1991).

Secondary Material

Adorno, Theodore, 'The schema of mass culture', in *The Culture Industry: Selected Essays on Mass Culture*, ed. J.M. Bernstein (London: Routledge, 1991).

Adorno, Theodore and Horkheimer, Max, *Dialectic of Enlightenment*, trans. John Cumming (London: Verso, 1979).

Aglietta, Michel, *A Theory of Capitalist Regulation: The US Experience*, trans. David Fernbach (London: New Left Books, 1979).

Angus, Ian, and Jhally, Sut (eds), *Cultural Politics in Contemporary America* (New York: Routledge, 1989).

Armstrong, Philip, Glyn, Andrew and Harrison, John, *Capitalism Since 1945* (Oxford: Basil Blackwell, 1991).

Arnold, Matthew, *Culture and Anarchy* (1869), ed. Samuel Lipman (New Haven: Yale University Press, 1994).

Aronowitz, Stanley, *The Crisis in Historical Materialism: Class, Politics and Culture in Marxist Theory* (Minneapolis: University of Minnesota Press, 1990).

—— *The Politics of Identity: Class, Culture, Social Movements* (London: Routledge, 1992).

Atlas, James, 'What is Fukuyama saying?', in *The New York Times*, 22 October 1989.

Bailey, Joe, *Pessimism* (London: Routledge, 1988).

Barthes, Roland, *Image – Music – Text*, trans. Stephen Heath (London: Fontana, 1977).

—— *The Fashion System*, trans. Matthew Ward and Richard Howard (London: Jonathan Cape, 1985).

—— *The Pleasure of the Text*, trans. Richard Miller (Oxford: Basil Blackwell, 1990).

Bataille, Georges, *The Story of the Eye* (1928), in Georges Bataille, *The Story of the Eye: With Essays by Susan Sontag and Roland Barthes*, trans. Joachim Neugroschel (London: Penguin, 1982).

—— *Visions of Excess: Selected Writing, 1927–1939*, ed. and introduced by Allan Stoekl, with Carol Lovitt and Donald Leslie (Manchester: Manchester University Press, 1985).

Baudelaire, Charles, *Les Fleurs du Mal* (1853), trans. Richard Howard (Brighton: Harvester, 1982).

—— *Les Paradis Artificiels: Opium et Haschisch* (Paris: Poulet-Malassis et de Broise, 1860).

—— 'The painter of modern life' (1863), in Charles Baudelaire, *The Painter of Modern Life and Other Essays*, ed. and trans. Jonathan Mayne (London: Phaidon, 1964).

Baudrillard, Jean, *Simulations*, trans. Paul Foss, Paul Patton and Philip Beitchman (New York: Semiotext(e), 1983).
—— *America*, trans. Chris Turner (London: Verso, 1988).
—— *Selected Writings*, ed. Mark Poster (Cambridge: Polity Press, 1988).
—— *Cool Memories*, trans. Chris Turner (London: Verso, 1990).
—— *Symbolic Exchange and Death*, trans. Iain Hamilton Grant (London: Sage, 1993).
Bazin, André , *What is Cinema?*, vol. 1, ed. and trans. Hugh Gray (California: University of California Press, 1967).
Beer, Gillian, 'Representing women: re-presenting the past', in Catherine Belsey and Jane Moore (eds), *The Feminist Reader: Essays in Gender and the Politics of Literary Criticism* (Houndmills: Macmillan, 1989).
Bell, Daniel, *The End of Ideology: On the Exhaustion of Political Ideas in the Fifties* (New York: The Free Press, 1965).
—— *The Coming of Post-Industrial Society: A Venture in Social Forecasting* (Harmondsworth: Penguin, 1976).
—— *The Cultural Contradictions of Capitalism*, 2nd ed. (London: Heinemann, 1979).
Benjamin, Walter, *Charles Baudelaire: A Lyric Poet in the Era of High-Capitalism*, trans. Harry Zohn (London: New Left Books, 1973).
—— *One-Way Street and Other Writings*, trans. Edmund Jephcott and Kingsley Shorter (London: New Left Books, 1979).
—— *Reflections: Essays, Aphorisms, Autobiographical Writings*, trans. Edmund Jephcott (New York: Schocken Books, 1986).
—— *Illuminations*, trans. Harry Zohn (London: Fontana, 1992).
Bennett, Tony, Mercer, Colin and Woollacott, Janet (eds), *Popular Culture and Social Relations* (Milton Keynes: Open University Press, 1986).
Berger, John, *Ways of Seeing* (London: BBC and Penguin, 1972).
Best, Stephen and Kellner, Douglas, *Postmodern Theory: Critical Interrogations* (Houndmills: Macmillan, 1991).
Birkett, Jennifer, *The Sins of the Fathers: Decadence in France, 1870–1914* (London: Quartet Books, 1986).
Bloch, Ernst (ed.), *Aesthetics and Politics*, translation editor Roland Taylor (London: New Left Books, 1977).
Boddy, Kasia, 'Conversations with Lynne Tillman', in *Overhere: Reviews in American Studies* (Summer 1994), vol. 14.1.
—— 'No innocent abroad: the fiction of Lynne Tillman', in *Overhere: Reviews in American Studies* (Summer 1994), vol. 14.1.
Bonefeld, Werner and Holloway, John (eds), *Post-Fordism and Social Form: A Marxist Debate on the Post-Fordist State* (Houndmills: Macmillan, 1991).
Bourdieu, Pierre, *Reproduction in Education, Society and Culture*, trans. Richard Nice (London: Sage, 1977).

—— *La Distinction: Critique Sociale du Jugement* (Paris: Les Editions de Minuit, 1979).

—— *Distinction: A Social Critique of the Judgement of Taste*, trans. Richard Nice (London: Routledge and Kegan Paul, 1984).

—— *Language and Symbolic Power*, ed. John Thompson, trans. Gino Raymond and Matthew Adamson, (Cambridge: Polity Press, 1991).

—— *The Field of Cultural Production: Essays on Art and Literature* (Cambridge: Polity Press, 1993).

Bourdieu, Pierre and Coleman, James (eds), *Social Theory for a Changing Society* (Boulder, Colorado: Westview, 1991).

Bowlby, Rachel, *Just Looking: Consumer Culture in Dreiser, Gissing and Zola* (London: Methuen, 1985).

—— *Still Crazy After All These Years: Women, Writing and Psychoanalysis* (London: Routledge, 1992).

—— *Shopping with Freud* (London: Routledge, 1993).

Braidwood, Phillipa, 'Tacky, tawdry and not fit for children', in *The Daily Express*, 22 October 1992.

Brantlinger, Patrick, *Bread and Circuses: Theories of Mass Culture and Social Decay* (Ithaca: Cornell University Press, 1983).

Bredbeck, Gregory, 'The new queer narrative: intervention and critique', in *Textual Practice* (Winter 1995), no. 9.3.

Brooker, Peter, *New York Fictions: Modernity, Postmodernism and the New Modern* (Essex: Longman, 1996).

Brooks, Peter, *Body Works: Objects of Desire in Modern Narrative* (Cambridge, Massachusetts: Harvard University Press, 1993).

Brown, Norman O., *Life Against Death: The Psychoanalytical Meaning of History*, 2nd ed. (Connecticut: Wesleyan University Press, 1985).

Buford, Bill, 'Introduction', in Bill Buford (ed.), *Granta: Dirty Realism – New Writing from America* (Cambridge: Granta, 1983), no. 8.

Burroughs, William, *Junky* (1953) (London: Penguin, 1977).

Butler, Judith, *Gender Trouble: Feminism and the Subversion of Identity* (London: Routledge, 1990).

—— *Bodies that Matter: On the Discursive Limits of 'Sex'* (London: Routledge, 1993).

Calinescu, Matei, *Faces of Modernity: Avant-Garde, Decadence, Kitsch* (Bloomington: Indiana University Press, 1977).

Campbell, Colin, *The Romantic Ethic and the Spirit of Modern Consumerism* (Oxford: Basil Blackwell, 1987).

Carey, James, *Communication as Culture: Essays on Media and Society* (Boston: Unwin Hyman, 1989).

Carey, James (ed.), *Media, Myths and Narratives: Television and the Press* (Newbury Park, California: Sage, 1988).

Certeau, Michel de, *The Practice of Everyday Life*, trans. Stephen Rendall (Berkeley: University of California Press, 1984).

Clarke, Roger, 'Scalpel on the soul', in The *Observer*, 27 March 1994.

—— 'Over their dead bodies', in The *Observer*, 25 September 1994.

Coe, Richard, *The Vision of Jean Genet* (London: Peter Owen, 1968).

Cohen, Joshua, 'Dying to watch TV: film, postmodernity, systems and DeLillo's *White Noise*', in *Overhere: Reviews in American Studies* (Summer 1993), vol. 13.1.

—— 'The look of the sight machine: Coover and the Question of Cinematic Vision', in *Diatribe* (Winter 1994/5), no. 4.

Comolli, Jean-Louis, 'Machines of the visible', in Stephen Heath and Teresa de Lauretis (eds), *The Cinematic Apparatus* (London: Macmillan, 1980).

Connor, Steven, *Postmodernist Culture: An Introduction to Theories of the Contemporary* (Oxford: Basil Blackwell, 1992).

—— *Theory and Cultural Value* (Oxford: Blackwell, 1992).

Cooper, Dennis (ed.), *Discontents: New Queer Writers* (New York: Amethyst Press, 1992).

Craft, Christopher, '"kiss me with those red lips": gender and inversion in Bram Stoker's *Dracula*', in Elaine Showalter (ed.), *Speaking of Gender*, (New York: Routledge, 1989).

Crook, Stephen, Pakulski, Jan and Waters, Malcolm, *Postmodernization: Change in Advanced Societies* (London: Sage, 1992).

D'Amico, Robert, 'Desire and the commodity form', in *Telos: A Quarterly Journal of Radical Thought* (Spring 1985), no. 35.

Davis, Mike, 'Urban renaissance and the spirit of postmodernism', in *New Left Review* (May/June 1985), no. 151.

—— *City of Quartz: Excavating the Future in Los Angeles* (London: Vintage, 1992).

Debord, Guy, *Comments on the Society of the Spectacle*, trans. Malcolm Imrie (London: Verso, 1990).

—— *The Society of the Spectacle*, trans. Donald Nicholson-Smith (New York: Zone, 1994).

Deleuze, Gilles and Sacher Masoch, Leopold von, *Masochism* (New York: Zone, 1989).

Dellamora, Richard, *Apocalyptic Overtures: Sexual Politics and the Sense of an Ending* (New Brunswick, New Jersey: Rutgers University Press, 1994).

Dijkstra, Bram, *Idols of Perversity: Fantasies of Feminine Evil in the Fin de Siècle* (Oxford: Oxford University Press, 1986).

Dowling, William, *Jameson, Althusser, Marx: An introduction to the Political Unconscious* (London: Methuen, 1984).

During, Simon, 'Postmodernism or postcolonialism today', in *Textual Practice* (1989), vol. 1.1.

162   *Blank Fictions*

Dyer, Richard, *Heavenly Bodies: Film Stars and Society* (Houndmills: Macmillan, 1986).
Eagleton, Terry, *Criticism and Ideology* (London: New Left Books, 1976).
—— *Marxism and Literary Criticism* (London: Methuen, 1976).
—— *Walter Benjamin, or, Towards a Revolutionary Criticism* (London: New Left Books, 1981).
—— 'Capitalism, modernism and postmodernism', in *New Left Review* (July/August 1985), no. 152.
—— *The Ideology of the Aesthetic* (Oxford: Blackwell, 1990).
Ehrenreich, Barbara and Ehrenreich, John, 'The professional managerial class', in Pat Walker (ed.), *Between Labour and Capital* (Brighton: Harvester, 1979).
Emerson, Ralph Waldo, 'Beauty' (1863), in Ralph Waldo Emerson, *The Collected Works of Ralph Waldo Emerson, Volume 1: Native Addresses and Lectures*, ed. Robert Spiller and Alfred Ferguson (Cambridge, Massachusetts: Belknap Press, 1971).
Evans, Julia, 'Shampoo Planet', in The *Guardian*, 6 April 1993.
Ewen, Stuart, *Captains of Consciousness: The Social Roots of Consumer Culture* (New York: McGraw Hill, 1976).
—— *All Consuming Images: The Politics of Style in Contemporary Culture* (New York: Basic Books, 1988).
Ewen, Stuart and Ewen, Elizabeth, *Channels of Desire: Mass Images and the Shaping of the American Consciousness* (New York: McGraw-Hill, 1982).
Featherstone, Mike, *Consumer Culture and Postmodernism* (London: Sage, 1991).
Featherstone, Mike, Hepworth, Mike and Turner, Bryan, (eds), *The Body: Social Process and Cultural Theory* (London: Sage, 1991).
Federman, Raymond (ed.), *Surfiction: Fiction Now ... and Tomorrow* (Chicago: The Swallow Press, 1975).
Feenberg, Andrew, *Lukács, Marx and the Sources of Critical Theory* (New York: Oxford University Press, 1981).
Fiske, John, *Power Plays, Power Works* (London: Verso, 1993).
Fitzgerald, F. Scott, *The Great Gatsby* (1926) (Harmondsworth: Penguin, 1984).
Fletcher, Ian, (ed.), *Decadence in the 1890s* (London: Edward Arnold, 1979).
Foster, Hal (ed.), *Postmodern Culture* (London: Pluto, 1987).
Fox, Richard and Jackson Lears, T.J. (eds), *The Culture of Consumption: Critical Essays in American History, 1880–1980* (New York: Pantheon, 1983).
Freese, Peter, 'Bret Easton Ellis, *Less Than Zero*: entropy in the "MTV novel"?', in Reingard Nishik and Barbara Korte (eds), *Modes of Narrative: Approaches to American, Canadian and British Fiction* (Wurzburg: Konighausen and Neumann, 1990).

French, Philip, 'Hell in Los Angeles', in The *Observer*, 23 October 1994.

Freud, Sigmund, *The Standard Edition of the Complete Psychological Works of Sigmund Freud*, translation editor James Strachey (London: Hogarth Press, 1961).

Frith, Simon, Goodwin, Andrew and Grossberg, Lawrence (eds), *Sound and Vision: The Music Video Reader* (London: Routledge, 1993).

Fukuyama, Francis, 'The end of history', in the *The National Interest* (Summer 1989), no. 16.

Galbraith, John Kenneth, *The Affluent Society* (1958), 4th ed. (London: Penguin, 1987).

Garnham, Nicholas and Williams, Raymond, 'Pierre Bourdieu and the sociology of culture', in Richard Collins *et al.* (eds), *Media, Culture and Society: A Critical Reader* (London: Sage, 1986).

Gee, Jack, 'Madonna: my book isn't porn', in the *Daily Express*, 12 October 1992.

Gerrard, Nicci, 'Bret and the beast in the corner', in the *Observer*, 16 October 1994.

Gitlin, Todd (ed.), *Watching Television* (New York: Pantheon, 1986).

Godden, Richard, *Fictions of Capital: The American Novel from James to Mailer* (Cambridge: Cambridge University Press, 1990).

Goldmann, Lucien, *The Hidden God: The Study of Tragic Vision in the Pensées of Pascal and the Tragedies of Racine*, trans. Philip Thody (London: Routledge and Kegan Paul, 1964).

—— *Towards a Sociology of the Novel*, trans. Alan Sheridan (London: Tavistock, 1975).

Gramsci, Antonio, *Selections from the Prison Notebooks of Antonio Gramsci*, trans. and ed. Quintin Hoare and Geoffrey Nowell Smith (London: Lawrence and Wishart, 1971).

Grant, Linda, *Sexing the Millennium: A Political History of the Sexual Revolution* (London: HarperCollins, 1993).

Grossberg, Lawrence, *We Gotta Get Out of This Place: Popular Conservatism and Postmodern Culture* (New York: Routledge, 1992).

Hardin, Rob, 'A dry ice stream from LA's womb of emptiness', in *American Book Review* (December 1993/January 1994), vol. 15.5.

Harraway, Donna, *Simians, Cyborgs and Women: The Reinvention of Nature* (London: Free Association Books, 1991).

Harvey, David, *The Limits of Capital* (Oxford: Basil Blackwell, 1982).

—— *The Condition of Postmodernity: An Enquiry into the Origins of Cultural Change* (Oxford: Blackwell, 1990).

Haug, W.F., *Critique of Commodity Aesthetics: Appearance, Sexuality and Advertising in Capitalist Society*, trans. Robert Boch (Cambridge: Polity Press, 1986).

Hebdidge, Dick, *Subcultures: The Meaning of Style* (London: Routledge, 1988).

—— *Hiding in the Light* (London: Routledge, 1988).

Heller, Agnes (ed.), *Lukács Reappraised* (New York: Columbia University Press, 1983).

Hobsbawm, Eric, *Industry and Empire* (Harmondsworth: Penguin, 1969).

—— *The Age of Capital: 1848–1875* (London: Weidenfeld and Nicolson, 1975).

—— *The Age of Empire: 1875–1914* (London: Weidenfeld and Nicolson, 1987).

Hutcheon, Linda, *A Poetics of Postmodernism: History, Theory, Fiction* (New York: Routledge, 1988).

Huysmans, Joris-Karl, *Against Nature* (1884), trans. Robert Baldick (Harmondsworth: Penguin, 1966).

Jackson, Earl, 'Death drives across porntopia: Dennis Cooper and the extremities of being', in *GLQ: A Journal of Lesbian and Gay Studies* (Summer 1993), no. 1.1.

Jameson, Fredric, *Marxism and Form: Twentieth Century Dialectical Theories of Literature* (Princeton, New Jersey: Princeton University Press, 1971).

—— 'The politics of theory: ideological positions in the postmodernism debate', in *New German Critique* (Fall 1984), no. 33.

—— 'Postmodernism, or, the cultural logic of late capitalism', in *New Left Review* (July/August 1984), no. 146.

—— *The Political Unconscious: Narrative as a Socially Symbolic Act* (London: Routledge, 1986).

—— 'Postmodernism and consumer society', in Hal Foster (ed.), *Postmodern Culture* (London: Pluto Press, 1987).

—— *The Ideologies of Theory: Essays 1971–1986, Volume 1: Situations of Theory* (London: Routledge, 1988).

—— *The Ideologies of Theory: Essays 1971–1986, Volume 2: The Syntax of History* (London: Routledge, 1988).

—— *Signatures of the Visible* (London: Routledge, 1990).

—— *The Geopolitical Aesthetic: Cinema and Space in the World System* (London: BFI, 1992).

—— *Postmodernism, or, The Cultural Logic of Late Capitalism* (London: Verso, 1993).

—— *The Seeds of Time* (New York: Columbia University Press, 1994).

Jay, Martin, *Fin-de-Siècle Socialism and Other Essays* (New York: Routledge, 1988).

—— *Downcast Eyes: The Denigration of Vision in Twentieth-Century French Thought* (Berkeley: University of California Press, 1993).

Juvenal, Decimus Junius, 'Satire X' (circa 125), in Decimus Junius Juvenal, *Sixteen Satires Upon the Ancient Harlot*, ed. and trans. Stephen Robinson (Manchester: Carcanet New Press, 1983).

Kadrey, Richard, *Covert Culture Sourcebook* (New York: St Martin's Press, 1993).

—— *Covert Culture Sourcebook 2.0* (New York: St Martin's Press, 1994).

Kaplan, E. Ann, *Rocking Around the Clock: Music Television, Postmodernism and Consumer Culture* (London: Methuen, 1987).

Keats, John, 'Ode on a Grecian urn', (1820) in John Keats, *The Poetical Writings and Other Works of John Keats*, ed. H. Buxton Foreman (New York: Charles Scribner's Sons, 1939), vol. 3.

Kellner, Douglas, 'TV, ideology and emancipatory popular culture', in Horace Newcomb (ed.), *Television: The Critical View*, 3rd ed. (New York: Oxford University Press, 1982).

—— *Jean Baudrillard: From Marxism to Postmodernism and Beyond* (Oxford: Polity, 1989).

—— *Television and the Crisis of Democracy* (Boulder: Westview, 1990).

Kellner, Douglas (ed.), *Postmodernism/Jameson/Critique* (Washington: Maissonneuve Press, 1989).

Kopkind, Andrew, 'Slacking toward Bethlehem', in *Grand Street* (1993), no. 44.

Kristeva, Julia, *Desire in Language: A Semiotic Approach to Literature and Art*, ed. Leon S. Roudiez, trans. Thomas Gora, Alice Jardine and Leon S. Roudiez, (Oxford: Basil Blackwell, 1980).

Kruger, Barbara, *Remote Control* (Cambridge, Massachusetts: MIT Press, 1993).

Landesman, Cosmo, 'The aristos of apathy', in the *Guardian*, 3 December 1992.

Lash, Scott, *Sociology of Postmodernism* (London: Routledge, 1990).

Lash, Scott and Urry, John, *The End of Organized Capitalism* (Cambridge: Polity Press, 1987).

Latimer, Dan, 'Jameson and postmodernism', in *New Left Review* (November/December 1984), no. 148.

Ledger, Sally and McCracken, Scott (eds), *Cultural Politics at the Fin de Siècle* (Cambridge: Cambridge University Press, 1995).

Lee, Martin, *Consumer Culture Reborn: The Cultural Politics of Consumption* (London: Routledge, 1993).

Lefbvre, Henri, *Critique of Everyday Life*, vol. 1, trans. John Moore (London: Verso, 1991).

Lehman, David, 'Two divine decadents', in *Newsweek*, 7 September 1987.

Levy, William, 'The diarist of circumstances', in *American Book Review* (December 1993/January 1994), vol. 15.5.

Lukács, Georg, *The Meaning of Contemporary Realism*, trans. John Mander and Necke Mander (London: Merlin Press, 1963).

—— *History and Class Consciousness: Studies in Marxist Dialectics*, trans. Rodney Livingstone (London: Merlin, 1971).

—— *The Historical Novel*, trans. Hannah Mitchell and Stanley Mitchell (Harmondsworth: Penguin, 1976).

—— *The Theory of the Novel: A Historico-Philosophical Essay on the Forms of Great Epic Literature*, trans. Anna Bostock (London: Merlin, 1978).

Lyotard, Jean-Francois, *The Postmodern Condition: A Report on Knowledge*, trans. Geoffrey Bennington and Brian Massumi (Manchester: Manchester University Press, 1984).

McCracken, Grant, *Culture and Consumption: New Approaches to the Symbolic Character of Consumer Goods and Activities* (Bloomington: Indiana University Press, 1988).

McHale, Brian, *Postmodernist Fiction* (New York: Methuen, 1987).

Madonna, *Sex* (London: Secker and Warburg, 1992).

Mailer, Norman, 'Children of the Pied Piper', in *Vanity Fair* (March 1991).

Malcolm, Derek, 'Drop-in for drop-outs', in the *Guardian*, 3 December 1992.

—— 'A cheap thrill a minute', in the *Guardian*, 20 October 1994.

Mandel, Ernest, *Late Capitalism*, trans. Joris de Bres (London: Verso, 1978).

—— *The Second Slump: A Marxist Analysis of Recession in the Seventies*, trans. Jan Rothschild (London: New Left Books 1978).

—— *Long Waves of Capitalist Development: The Marxist Interpretation* (Cambridge: Cambridge University Press, 1980).

Marcuse, Herbert, *One-Dimensional Man: Studies in the Ideology of Advanced Industrial Society* (London: Ark, 1986).

—— *Negations: Essays in Critical Theory*, trans. Jeremy Shapiro (London: Free Association Books, 1988).

Mark, M. (ed.), *Disorderly Conduct: The VLS Fiction Reader* (London: Serpent's Tail, 1991).

Marx, Karl, *Capital*, vol. 1, trans. Ben Fowkes (Harmondsworth: Penguin Books, 1976).

—— *Capital*, vol. 2, trans. David Fernbach (Harmondsworth: Penguin, 1978).

—— *Capital*, vol. 3, trans. David Fernbach (Harmondsworth: Penguin, 1981).

Mascia-Lees, Frances and Sharpe, Patricia (eds), *Tattoo, Torture, Mutilation and Adornment: The Denaturalization of the Body in Culture and Text* (New York: State University of New York Press, 1992).

Messud, Claire, 'Nightmare on Mean Street', in the *Guardian*, 20 April 1996.

Mestrovic, Stjepan, *The Coming Fin de Siècle: An Application of Durkheim's Sociology to Modernity and Postmodernism* (London: Routledge, 1991).

Meyrowitz, Joshua, *No Sense of Place: The Impact of Electronic Media on Social Behaviour* (New York: Oxford University Press, 1985).

Minc, Alain, *Le Nouveau Moyen Âge* (Paris: Gallimard, 1993).

Moers, Ellen, *The Dandy: Brummell to Beerbohm* (London: Secker and Warburg, 1960).

Mulvey, Laura, 'Visual pleasure and narrative cinema', in *Screen* (Autumn 1975), vol. 16.3.

Nelson, Cary and Grossberg, Lawrence (eds), *Marxism and the Interpretation of Culture* (Houndmills and London: Macmillan, 1988).

Nelson, Emmanuel (ed.), *Contemporay Gay American Novelists: A Bio-Biographical Critical Sourcebook* (Westport, Connecticut: Greenwood Press, 1993).

Nicholls, Peter, *Modernisms: A Literary Guide* (London: Macmillan, 1995).

—— 'A conversation with Lynne Tillman', in *Textual Practice* (1995), no. 9.2.

Nye, David, and Pederson, Carl (eds), *Consumption and American Culture* (Amsterdam: VU University Press, 1991).

O'Connor, James, *Accumulation Crisis* (New York: Basil Blackwell, 1984).

Offe, Claus, *Disorganized Capitalism: Contemporary Transformations of Work and Politics*, ed. John Keane (Cambridge: Polity Press, 1985).

Olalquiaga, Celeste, *Megalopolis: Contemporary Cultural Sensibilities* (Minneapolis: University of Minnesota Press, 1992).

Owens, Craig, *Beyond Recognition: Representation, Power and Culture*, ed. Scott Bryson, Barabara Kruger, Lynne Tillman and Jane Weinstock, introduced by Simon Watney (Los Angeles: University of California Press, 1992).

Packard, Vance, *The Hidden Persuaders*, 2nd ed. (Harmondsworth: Penguin, 1981).

Pan, David, 'Wishing for more', in *Telos: A Quarterly Journal of Critical Thought* (Summer 1988), no. 76.

Parfrey, Adam (ed.), *Apocalypse Culture*, expanded and revised ed. (Los Angeles: Feral House, 1990).

Pater, Walter, *The Renaissance: Studies in Art and Literature* (1873), ed. Adam Philips (Oxford: Oxford University Press, 1986).

Paulson, William, *The Noise of Culture: Literary Texts in a World of Information* (Ithaca: Cornell University Press, 1968).

Perrin, Stephen, 'Chasing the dragon: the junky as 20th century hero', in *Overhere: Reviews in American Studies* (Summer 1993), no. 13.1.

Petit, Chris, 'The hippest nerd in the movies', in the *Guardian*, 28 July 1995.

Pfeil, Fred, *Another Tale to Tell: Politics and Narrative in Postmodern Culture* (London: Verso, 1990).

Plant, Sadie, *The Most Radical Gesture: The Situationist International in a Postmodern Age* (London: Routledge, 1992).

Poster, Mark, *The Mode of Information: Poststructuralism and Social Context* (Oxford: Polity Press, 1990).

Powell, Anna, 'Tripping the dark fantastic', in *Metropolitan* (Winter 1995/6).

Preteceille, Edmond and Terrail, Jean-Pierre, *Capitalism, Consumption and Needs*, trans. Sarah Matthews (Oxford: Basil Blackwell, 1985).

Reynolds, Simon and Press, Joy, *The Sex Revolts: Gender, Rebellion and Rock n' Roll* (Cambridge, Massachusetts: Harvard University Press, 1995).

Richler, Noah, 'Firing with blanks', in the *Guardian*, 24 November 92.

Rosenblatt, Roger, 'Snuff this book', in *The New York Times*, 16 December 1990.

Ross, Andrew (ed.), *Universal Abandon: The Politics of Postmodernism* (Edinburgh: Edinburgh University Press, 1989).

Rudgely, Richard, *The Alchemy of Culture: Intoxicants in Society* (London: British Museum Press, 1993).

Rushcoff, Douglas (ed.), *The GenX Reader* (New York: Ballantine Books, 1994).

Sahlin, Nicki, '"But this road doesn't go anywhere": the existential dilemma in *Less Than Zero*', in *Critique: Studies in Contemporary Fiction* (Fall 1991), no. 33.

Schreiber, Flora Rhita, *The Shoemaker: Anatomy of a Psychotic* (London: Allen Lane, 1983).

Seltzer, Mark, *Bodies and Machines* (London: Routledge, 1992).

Senf, Carol, *The Vampire in Nineteenth Century English Literature* (Bowling Green: Popular Press, 1988).

Shaviro, Steven, *Passion and Excess: Blanchot, Bataille, and Literary Theory* (Tallahassee: Florida State University Press, 1990).

Shields, Rob (ed.), *Lifestyle Shopping: The Subject of Consumption* (London: Routledge, 1992).

Shnayerson, Michael, 'Women behaving badly', in *Vanity Fair* (February 1997).

Showalter, Elaine, *Sexual Anarchy: Gender and Culture at the Fin de Siècle* (London: Bloomsbury, 1991).

Siegle, Robert, *Suburban Ambush: Downtown Writing and the Fiction of Insurgency* (Baltimore: Johns Hopkins University Press, 1989).

Sinai, Robert, *The Decadence of the Modern World* (Cambridge, Massachusetts: Schekman, 1978).

Sipchen, Bob, 'Big hitters gun for Hollywood', in the *Guardian*, 13 June 1995.

Soja, Edward, *Postmodern Geographies: The Reassertion of Space and Time in Critical Social Theory* (London: Verso, 1989).

Speigel, Alan, *Fiction and the Camera Eye* (Virginia: University of Virginia, 1976).

Spivak, Gayatri, 'The decadent style', in *Language and Style* (1974), vol. 7.

Stokes, John (ed.), *Fin de Siècle/Fin de Globe: Fears and Fantasies of the Late Nineteenth Century* (Houndmills: Macmillan, 1992).

Strausbaugh, John and Blaise, Donald (eds), *The Drug User: Documents 1840–1960* (New York: Blast Books, 1991).

Synnott, Anthony, *The Body Social: Symbolism, Self and Society* (London: Routledge, 1993).

Teich, Mikulas and Porter, Roy (eds), *Fin de Siècle and its Legacy* (Cambridge: Cambridge University Press, 1990).

Thornton, R.K.R., *The Decadent Dilemma* (London: Edward Arnold, 1983).

Tillman, Lynne, 'Critical fiction/critical self', in Philomena Mariani (ed.), *Critical Fictions: The Politics of Imaginative Writing* (Seattle: Bay Press, 1991).

—— 'To find words', in Alison Fell (ed.), *Serious Hysterics* (London: Serpent's Tail, 1992).

Touraine, Alain, *The Post-Industrial Society: Tomorrow's Social History – Classes, Conflicts and Culture in a Programmed Society*, trans. Leonard Mayhew (London: Wildwood House, 1974).

Turner, Bryan, *The Body and Society: Explorations in Social Theory* (Oxford: Basil Blackwell, 1984).

Twitchell, James, *The Living Dead: A Study of the Vampire in Romantic Literature* (Durham, North Carolina: Duke University Press 1981).

Tyler, Andrew, *Street Drugs*, 2nd ed. (Sevenoaks, Kent: Hodder and Stoughton, 1988).

Tyrnauer, Matthew, 'Who's afraid of Bret Easton Ellis?', in *Vanity Fair* (August 1994).

Urry, John, *The Tourist Gaze: Leisure and Travel in Contemporary Societies* (London: Sage, 1990).

Varma, Devendra, 'The genesis of Dracula: a re-visit', in Margaret Carter (ed.), *Dracula: The Vampire and the Critics* (Ann Arbor: UMI Research Press, 1988).

Veblen, Thorstein, 'The economic theory of woman's dress', in *The Popular Science Monthly*, (December 1894), no. 46.

——— 'Editorial from *The Dial*', 14 June 1919, in Thorstein Veblen, *Essays on Our Changing Order*, ed. Leon Ardzrooni (New York: Viking, 1934).

——— *The Theory of The Leisure Class: An Economic Study of Institutions* (1899) (London: Unwin Books, 1970).

Vološinov, V.N., *Marxism and the Philosophy of Language*, trans. Ladislav Matejka and I.R. Tutnick (New York: Seminar Press, 1973).

Wallis, Brian, 'An absence of vision and drama', in *Parkett* (1985), vol. 5.

Walsh, John, 'Accessories before the fact', in the *Sunday Times*, 21 April 1991.

Waugh, Patricia, *Metafiction: The Theory and Practice of Self-Conscious Fiction* (London: Methuen, 1984).

Webster, Duncan, *Looka Yonder! The Imaginary America of Popularist Culture* (London: Comedia, 1988).

West, Nathanael, *The Day of the Locust* (1939), in Nathanael West, *The Day of the Locust and the Dream Life of Balso Snell* (London: Penguin, 1991).

West, Shearer, *Fin de Siècle* (London: Bloomsbury, 1993).

Whissen, Thomas Reed, *The Devil's Advocates: Decadence in Modern Literature* (New York: Greenwood, 1989).

Wicke, Jennifer, *Advertising Fictions: Literature, Advertisement and Social Reading* (New York: Columbia, 1988).

Wilde, Oscar, *The Picture of Dorian Gray* (1890), in Oscar Wilde, *Plays, Prose Writings and Poems*, introduced by Isobel Murray (London: Dent, 1975).

Williams, Linda, *Hard Core: Power, Pleasure and the 'Frenzy of the Visible'* (London: Pandora, 1991).

Williams, Rosalind, *Dream Worlds: Mass Consumption in Late Nineteenth-Century France* (Berkeley: University of California Press, 1982).

Williamson, Judith, *Decoding Advertisements* (London: Marion Boyars, 1978).

Wordsworth, William, *The Prelude* (1805), in William Wordsworth, *The Prelude: A Parallel Text*, ed. J.C. Maxwell (London: Penguin, 1988).

Young, Elizabeth, 'And a good fang too', in the *Independent on Sunday*,13 March 1994).

——— 'Lost boy', in the *Guardian*, 1 October 1994.

Young, Elizabeth and Caveney, Graham, *Shopping in Space: Essays on American 'Blank Generation' Fiction* (London: Serpent's Tail, 1992).

Zaller, Robert, '*American Psycho*, American censorship and the Dahmer case', in *Revue Français D'Etudes Américaines* (July 1993), no. 57.

Index